W9-BII-684

FLORIDA STATE
UNIVERSITY LIBRARIES

DEC 2 1996

TALLAHASSEE, FLORIDA

Economic Incentives and Bilateral Cooperation

Economic Incentives
and Bilateral Cooperation

WILLIAM J. LONG

Ann Arbor

THE UNIVERSITY OF MICHIGAN PRESS

*HC
79
T4
L66
1996*

Copyright © by the University of Michigan 1996
All rights reserved
Published in the United States of America by
The University of Michigan Press
Manufactured in the United States of America
⊚ Printed on acid-free paper

1999   1998   1997   1996   4   3   2   1

No part of this publication may be reproduced, stored in a retrieval system, or transmitted in any form or by any means, electronic, mechanical, or otherwise without the written permission of the publisher.

A CIP catalog record for this book is available from the British Library.

Library of Congress Cataloging-in-Publication Data

Long, William J., 1956–
    Economic incentives and bilateral cooperation / William J. Long.
        p.   cm.
    Includes bibliographical references and index.
    ISBN 0-472-10747-X (hc : alk. paper)
    1. Technology transfer—Economic aspects.   2. International trade.
    3. International economic relations.   4. International cooperation.
    I. Title.
    HC79.T4L66   1996
    338'.064—dc20   96-25639
                                                               CIP

For Katie and Alex, my favorite teachers

Contents

Preface

The repeated use of economic incentives in response to post–Cold War problems in international relations sparked my interest in this topic. Motivated perhaps by the declining utility of military means, policymakers and pundits habitually recommend economic incentives as the solution to problems as diverse as nuclear weapons proliferation and rain forest depletion. Yet, I discovered that, despite their considerable attention to the role of economic sanctions in international politics, scholars have provided little insight into how economic incentives operate as a policy instrument. Part of the explanation for the absence of theoretical work on economic incentives may lie in the realist predilection for defining state power in coercive terms and the liberal bias of seeing economic relations as a function of apolitical market forces rather than as instruments of state influence. Whatever the reason, the combination of popular enthusiasm for, and scholarly neglect of, programmatic economic incentives means this important and increasingly prevalent policy instrument is poorly or incompletely understood.

This book attempts to contribute to a better understanding of the role of economic incentives in interstate cooperation. It is less concerned with engaging in the debate over *whether* economic incentives can foster bilateral cooperation. Rather, assuming that conflict and cooperation are both possible in international relations, it asks: *how* might incentives alter a state's external payoff environment and affect its internal preferences and choices so as to produce cooperative adjustment in its policies? Chapter 2 of this book offers an answer.

To inform my theoretical investigation and to derive general policy insights about incentives, I investigate three historical incentive cases in chapters 3, 4, and 5. Drawing on these cases and the theory of incentives offered in chapter 2, this book considers a second important area of inquiry of particular relevance to policymakers: *when* are incentives likely to induce cooperation, and what factors contribute to or detract from their practical success? I offer my conclusions regarding the necessary and supportive factors for a successful incentive policy in chapter 6. The book concludes with suggestions for further research into the theory and practice of economic incentives.

The theoretical insights and policy recommendations contained in this book have benefited from numerous insights from colleagues and reviewers. In addition, I am grateful to those practitioners and scholars whose expertise helped me understand U.S. incentive policies and the foreign policy responses of Sweden, China, and the former Czechoslovakia.

The author and the University of Michigan Press gratefully acknowledge the copyright lease of Blackwell Publishers for any material appearing as an article, "Trade and Technology Incentives and Bilateral Cooperation," in *International Studies Quarterly*.

I received financial and administrative support for this work from the Hewlett Foundation and the Consortium for Multi-Party Conflict Resolution, the Fulbright Commission, the Georgia Tech Foundation, the Swedish Institute, and the School of International Affairs of the Georgia Institute of Technology. I also greatly appreciate the research support of Kim Wildner and the careful manuscript preparation of Joy Daniell.

As always, I owe a special thanks to my wife, Mary, for her moral support and encouragement.

CHAPTER 1

Introduction

Can the United States or other countries meet their post–Cold War security challenges through economic incentives and expanded commercial exchange? How can policymakers use market access and technology transfer to build stable long-term cooperative relations with other countries? These are timely questions. Today one cannot open a newspaper without encountering a policymaker or analyst calling for the extension of a trade or technology incentive as a strategy for addressing foreign policy challenges. Incentives have been prescribed for diverse problems including staunching the flow of weapons expertise and materials from the countries of the former Soviet Union, dissuading North Korea from developing nuclear weapons or convincing Ukraine to destroy them, encouraging developing nations to adopt less environmentally dangerous economic policies, or coping with new security threats such as drug trafficking or immigration.

Unfortunately, international relations scholars have seldom considered the operation and possible uses of programmatic economic incentives as a means of international influence despite numerous studies of economic sanctions. The result of this imbalance is a well-developed body of theory and evidence on the operation of sanctions but little appreciation for the mechanics or effects of incentives outside the narrow context of tit-for-tat negotiating strategies.

Consequently, analysts have often assumed that programmatic incentives operate like sanctions, albeit weak ones. In one sense this is correct. Both incentives and sanctions offer the recipient (target) a new bargain. With incentives the sender is offering new or additional gains from trade, technology transfer, or capital for a desired policy adjustment by the recipient. In a sanction case, the sender is trying to collect a political concession for a threatened or actual withdrawal of economic gains it previously extended. Because the reallocation costs associated with the loss of existing trade are likely to exceed those associated with new trade and because the marginal utility of a benefit foregone necessarily exceeds that of an equal amount of new gain, one could conclude that incentives are merely weak relatives of sanctions.

Unfortunately, this conclusion ignores many important differences between the two instruments and limits our understanding of incentives. The goal of this book is to improve our understanding of the operation of economic incentives in international relations. This study examines three pertinent historical incentive cases: first, to develop a theory of how trade and technology incentives might work to affect interstate cooperation, and second, to provide some conditional generalizations for policymakers regarding when incentives work and the factors that enhance or limit their success. Beginning in chapter 2 the book offers a set of hypotheses on how incentives work to affect the prospects for bilateral cooperation. It explains the way incentives can foster bilateral cooperation both by changing the external environment facing states and by altering the domestic political determinants of a state's policy preferences.

The book then considers three historical incentive cases in chapters 3, 4, and 5. The cases include: (1) the transfer of U.S. civilian nuclear technology and materials to Sweden during the 1950s and 1960s to discourage Sweden's development of nuclear weapons manufacturing capabilities; (2) the exchange of U.S. trade, technology, and other economic benefits to the People's Republic of China (PRC) during the 1970s and 1980s in return for improved Sino-American political/strategic cooperation; and (3) the extension of most favored nation (MFN) tariff treatment, preferential financing, and access to advanced technology to Czechoslovakia during the early 1990s in exchange for cooperation in controlling the proliferation of weapons of mass destruction. The purpose of the cases is to inform and illustrate the theory of incentives through systematic empirical research.

This book also claims a degree of practical relevance to policymakers. Having explained the general logic behind the operation of economic incentives and considered their operation in several situations, in chapter 6 it makes some policy-relevant generalizations of when incentives might work and what factors contribute to, or detract from, their effectiveness. The concluding chapter summarizes the findings and makes suggestions for further research.

Before beginning the theoretical explanation of incentives, this introductory chapter describes the independent variable: trade and technology incentives offered by one state to an actual or potential recipient. It then specifies the dependent variables: state preferences and bilateral cooperation. The chapter also discusses applicable theoretical insights about interstate cooperation and preference formation that are necessary to understanding the operation and effects of incentives. Finally, the case study methodology is introduced.

The Independent Variable: Trade and Technology Incentives

Trade and technology incentives are a mode of power exercised through the promise or giving of an economic benefit to induce a state to change its political behavior in another area. They contrast significantly with denial strategies of varying comprehensiveness, which aim to force a change in the target's behavior by impeding the welfare or viability of the target state. In some cases, a state offers these forms of economic incentive with the intent of creating a commonality of interests or purposes between itself and another state and conditioning the outlook and choices of the recipient in a directed, but not direct or immediate, manner. These incentive programs involve the exchange of benefits or the promise to exchange benefits over a protracted period to create conditions that encourage a recipient's conformance with a desired standard of political behavior.[1] The policies examined are medium to long term and, although not overtly "coercive,"[2] clearly aim to influence the recipient state's behavior in a preferred direction.

States can also use economic inducements or rewards such as trade or technology transfer more directly as a specific, short-term benefit exchanged for an explicitly delineated response from the recipient. Although the distinctions between forms of economic incentives are matters of degree, not design, sender states employ trade and technology incentives in this latter case more precisely to elicit specific and near-term alterations in a recipient state's behavior. Such policies are more intimately connected with the alternating use of negative measures in a leveraging or negotiating processes. In popular parlance, these incentives are the "carrots" in "carrot-and-stick" diplomacy and are the form of cooperative incentive considered by most game theorists. A body of international relations theory discusses the short-term use of incentives as a bargaining and signaling device.[3] This book, however, focuses on long-term incentive strategies where the expected recipient response need not be immediate and matching but may be more diffuse. These programmatic forms of incentives are significant tools of state's foreign policies; with the exception of foreign aid, however, they have not been extensively examined.

Programmatic trade and technology transfer are an important, yet by no means the only important, form of economic incentives available to states to employ or to scholars to study. Their practical versatility, theoretical distinctiveness, and relative scholarly neglect, however, make them the focus here. Trade incentives can include tariff benefits achieved through the reduction of tariff rates toward, to, or below the most favored nation standard of the General Agreement on Tariffs and Trade (GATT).

Trade incentive policies can also take the form of a direct purchase, the granting of a government export or import license, or the promise to do any of the aforementioned.[4] The granting of a preferential trading arrangement, such as acquiescing to a commodity agreement, is another transfer of resources through trade. Technological benefits can occur through government policies that permit or facilitate the exchange of scientists or engineers, the export of a turnkey plant, or the transfer of disembodied technology (such as a computer code or other intellectual property). In capital transfer, incentives include not only foreign aid but also investment guarantees, encouragement of private or public multilateral capital exports, favorable taxation treatment, the creation and distribution of special drawing rights to developing countries, loan forgiveness, outright grants, and more.[5] As a practical matter, states often combine various forms of economic incentives as part of a broader program.

As noted, the focus of this study is on long-term economic incentives with a strong trade and technology component rather than on short-term incentives or grants-in-aid. The use of short-term incentives in the context of negotiations or in assessing direct reciprocal relations has been the subject of study within the negotiation and game theory literature, to the exclusion of more protracted influence attempts. Foreign aid has already received considerable scholarly and professional attention, while other incentive policies have gone largely unnoticed.[6] The emphasis on foreign aid as the only important form of incentive power is unfortunate. As discussed in chapter 2, foreign aid operates somewhat differently from trade and technology transfer as a theoretical matter, and, as a policy tool, economic rewards in the form of foreign aid have shrunk as a percentage of national income for many countries and have become an increasingly circumscribed policy instrument.[7] As discussed in chapter 6, trade and technology incentives are widely available and often-employed instruments whose attractiveness and use as a policy measure may be increasing. America's recent relations with Ukraine, Vietnam, China, North Korea, and Haiti are but a few examples. Therefore, the case studies under consideration focus on policies where the sender offers a material benefit to the recipient (in these instances, predominantly technology and trade benefits rather than aid) in the expectation of more cooperative political relations over time (as opposed to a specific, short-term reaction from the recipient).

Scholars have paid limited attention to the role of programmatic trade and technology incentives in international relations,[8] despite considerable interest in the coercive uses of trade and technology in the form of sanctions or boycotts.[9] International relations theorists typically discount the use and potential of trade and technology incentives as a tool of foreign policy. Many ignore incentives or dismiss them on theoretical grounds as power relations between states.[10] Other analysts, while acknowledging that, theoretically, they should include trade and technology inducements as a means by which states pursue their goals and affect the behavior of other actors or their environment, argue on practical grounds that these forms of economic incentives are of limited significance. They dismiss the availability of economic rewards for capitalist states, noting, for example, the difficulty of directing trade for political purposes in such societies and the general prohibitions against the use of selective preferences in trade for those market societies that are members of GATT.[11] Ironically, GATT recognizes the extension of nonreciprocal trade benefits such as the generalized system of preferences (GSP), and states have often tied the extension or removal of GSP treatment (or MFN treatment) to political concessions. As a general point, this depoliticization of trade approach fails to recognize that, while private actors carry out trade, "Attempts by statesmen to influence the pattern of international trade through manipulating this legal and political framework can be regarded as acts of economic statecraft."[12] Policies that create the possibility for international exchange, alter the terms of exchange, or enhance the technological capabilities of others are pervasive and powerful features of international relations worthy of investigation.

As a policy matter, states often employ trade or technology transfer measures to strengthen an ally or decrease the dependency or vulnerability of a potential ally or friend to a common adversary. States offer trade and technology incentives in varying forms to foster a preferred form of economic development, to instigate or promote particular values or interests in the recipient, or to create conditions for the provision of a collective good. Public policy that makes economic benefits possible is an example of an economic incentive that could increase another country's gains from trade or enhance its level of technology and shape its interests and policies. The prevalence of incentives and, as discussed subsequently, their relevance to issues of bilateral cooperation and state preference formation and change make incentives important objects of study.

To illustrate the point, the potential uses of just one form of economic incentive—civilian technology transfer—go far beyond the cases considered here. Limits on high technology transfer, a common American policy instrument during the Cold War, now serve as bases for trade and technology incentives. During the Cold War era, the United States had an extensive peacetime technology transfer regime that denied strategic American technology to communist countries and controlled the exchange of strategic and nonstrategic items for other reasons, including the promotion of human rights, the control of international terrorism, and the prevention of nuclear, biological, and chemical weapons, or ballistic missile proliferation.[13] Thus, as the denial of trade benefits grew as a foreign economic policy weapon, so grew the opportunity to relax or remove such restrictions as a means of influence. In Baldwin's words, "Today's reward may lay the groundwork for tomorrow's threat, and tomorrow's threat may lay the groundwork for a promise the day after tomorrow."[14] In the post–Cold War era, the affirmative transfer of technology to former adversaries has become an extremely important policy instrument. The United States, for example, is using trade and technology incentives to shape political and economic policies in the successor states to the Soviet Union and throughout Central and Eastern Europe and is exploring its use with other countries including Vietnam, North Korea, and Cuba.

The Dependent (and Interdependent) Variables

This study considers the question, "How can economic incentives (trade and technology) offered over time induce bilateral cooperation, that is, shape preferences and actions of the recipient in a manner consistent with the sender's intent?" Before addressing the role of incentives (the independent variable) in chapter 2, I focus first on the dependent variables, the issues to be explained.

Because incentives influence both international behavior and domestic politics, my hypotheses on economic incentives include variables at the level of both the international structure and the agents (states) that comprise it. Alexander Wendt argues that agents and social structures are, in one way or another, "theoretically interdependent or mutually implicating entities." He goes on to state, "It is then a plausible step to believe that the properties of agents and those of social structures are both relevant to explanations of social behavior."[15] Consistent with Wendt's approach, there are both structural and agent-level dependent variables in this study—bilateral cooperation and domestic policy preferences—and these dependent variables are themselves interdependent. The advantage of this approach is that neither state agents nor the international structure in which they operate is treated as a given; they are both causally relevant. This distinction is important because theories at the level of structure and theories at the level of agents explain different things. As David Dessler argues, "Structure alone explains only the possibilities (and impossibilities) of action,"[16] that is, "How is action x possible?"[17] Agent-level theories explain a particular outcome or choice of action, that is, "Why did x happen rather than y?"[18] Similarly, Robert Keohane writes that "asking why an actor behaved in a certain way is equivalent to asking what its incentives were: that is, what were the opportunity costs of its various alternative courses of action? Opportunity costs are determined by the nature of the environment as well as by the characteristics of the actor."[19] In explaining the impact of incentives on state action, therefore, this book will employ theoretical understandings of both system and agents.

For this study, at the level of the international system, the dependent variable is bilateral cooperation. The analysis focuses on how incentives affect the international environment for bilateral cooperation or noncooperation. This project adopts Keohane's definition: "cooperation" means the existence of a degree of *policy coordination* where "actors adjust their behavior to the actual or anticipated preferences of others."[20] Cooperation requires that a state adjust its policies to reduce the negative consequences on, or facilitate the goals of, another state.[21] The adjustment may be adaptive and need not involve formal bargaining or negotiation. Keohane contrasts cooperation with discord and harmony. Discord is the clash of states' policies without adjustment. Harmony is "a situation in which actors' policies (pursued for their own self-interest without regard for others) *automatically* facilitate the attainment of others' goals."[22] In harmony, states are not required to adjust their policy because of another state's interest.[23]

At the national or agent level, the dependent variable is state policy preference. This book adopts Terry Moe's approach to defining actors' preferences. He rejects goals such as "utility maximization" or "security" as too unspecified and undirected. Rather, substantively defined actor preferences "are more proximate to policy, and they are inevitably context-dependent."[24] Clearly, state policy preference formation and change are central to interstate cooperation. Indeed, the definition of cooperation offered by Keohane incorporates this national-level variable within it. As Andrew Moravcsik explains, "rationality suggests that parsimonious explanations of international conflict or cooperation can be constructed by employing two types of theory sequentially: a theory of national preference formation *and* a theory of interstate strategic interaction."[25] In short, explaining how incentives alter behavior requires an understanding of their impact on strategic interaction *and* how they alter national preferences.

Before assessing how incentives may influence state preferences and shape interstate strategic interaction in chapter 2, we need to consider where state preferences for cooperation come from and how they are altered. Several theories at the level of the international system and the level of state actors help us understand the possibility for cooperative behavior between states and sources of state preferences and how state preferences change. The next sections briefly review that literature. In the next chapter, I use these theoretical frameworks to generate hypotheses on the process by which incentives alter the international payoff structure facing states and how they shape preferences within states.

Structural Theories on the Possibility of Interstate Cooperation and State Preferences

The untempered realist model of international relations discounts the possibilities of cooperation. It views states as preoccupied with their own security; states are predisposed to competition and conflict rather than cooperation. States must act as individual agents in a hostile international system. In its most strident form, realism maintains that the barriers to cooperation are twofold. First, the chance that a potential partner would cheat or defect from a cooperative arrangement, conceivably costing the state its independence and survival, prevents a state from joint action. Second, even assuming a state could assure another's compliance, the fear that a partner's gain from cooperation will exceed its own and leave it relatively less powerful inhibits a state's willingness to cooperate. States, realists claim, will not cooperate short of a shared imminent threat because of enforcement problems and their concern over the relative achievement of gains.[26] Such cooperation is short-lived as individual national interests soon diverge and conflict returns or a state quickly turns the mechanisms for cooperation to enhancing its share of the benefits of joint action.

Not surprisingly, this approach limits the attention economic incentives, as a means toward cooperative relations, have received. Two generations of realist scholars of international relations have roundly discredited the notion that the benefits of commercial transactions and economic exchange can overcome the problem of international anarchy and conflict and foster cooperation.[27] Realists cite the outbreak of war in Europe in 1914 and Japan's attack on the United States (its most important trading partner) in 1941 as dramatic evidence that states pursue self-help and security interests unconstrained by an existing web of commercial contact between them.[28] Thus, the realist focus has been on statecraft defined largely as the pursuit of "power" conceived as "essentially military capability—the elements which contribute directly or indirectly to the capacity to coerce, kill, or destroy" or negative economic coercion.[29]

State preferences or the possibility that changes in preferences might alter interstate behavior are not prominent elements of the realist model. Rather, realist theory (especially the structural version) focuses on strategic interaction between states, not on changes within them. Realists derive state preferences from the distribution of power across the international system. States are generally presumed to be unitary, rational actors that will seek to increase national power and maintain a balance of power within the system.[30]

The liberal tradition in international relations has taken a more optimistic view of the possibility for interstate cooperation, often in sharp contrast to the realists.[31] Some liberal approaches to international relations have questioned the exclusive focus on states as actors seeking power and security under anarchic international conditions. At the core, however, liberals diverge from realists in their understanding of state motivations. Drawing an analogy from market economics, liberals argue that even states operating without centralized political authority can cooperate. States, if fully informed of their interests and those of other actors, will seek to increase their individual gains through mutually rewarding interactions rather than engage in unrewarding competition or outright conflict. The barriers to bilateral cooperation concern facilitation—avoiding misperception and miscalculation (recognizing the costs of conflict)—and enforcement (reducing the attractiveness of cheating, for example). Neoliberal approaches often suggest that states can overcome or mitigate these problems through the intervention of regimes or institutions.[32]

In their more sophisticated forms, liberal theories see state preferences as the result of interaction among states and domestic politics. Liberals, however, place particular emphasis on the role of regimes,[33] transnational contacts, and international laws and norms as factors shaping a state's preference for cooperation.[34]

In an attempt to bridge the realist-liberal gap on cooperation theory, political theorists, borrowing from behavioral scientists, have observed that subjects under controlled conditions may reciprocate the cooperative acts of their opponents in a tit-for-tat pattern. The works of Robert Axelrod[35] and Robert Keohane,[36] in particular, have drawn attention to the role of this form of direct reciprocity as a means for understanding cooperation among states.

Game theory often is the framework for incorporating the role of reciprocity in international relations. Some game theorists argue that individual states, without a central authority to enforce agreements, face mixed interests or motives that correspond with games such as Prisoner's Dilemma.[37] That game suggests that, in discrete interactions, state preferences will prohibit cooperation.[38] Specifically, Prisoner's Dilemma presents a 2×2 game, where two players each with two options—cooperation (C) or defection (noncooperation) (D)—illustrate points about international relations. This stylized approach creates four potential outcomes for each player, including mutual cooperation (C,C), mutual defection (D,D), unilateral defection (D,C), and unreciprocated cooperation (C,D). In relations with another state, Prisoner's Dilemma further assumes that each state prefers an outcome of mutual cooperation (C, C) to mutual defection (D, D). However, each state also presumably seeks its advantage by defecting while the other cooperates (D, C) to an outcome of mutual cooperation (C, C), and each state would prefer mutual defection (D, D) to a situation in which it is exploited by cooperating while the other state defects (C, D). Thus, the assumed preference order of states becomes: $DC > CC > DD > CD$.

As Robert Jervis notes, "What makes this configuration disturbing is that even if each side prefers CC to DD (and each knows that this is the other's preference), the result can be noncooperation (D,D) because each party is driven by the hope of gaining its first choice—which would be to exploit the other (D,C)—and its fear that, if it cooperates, the other will exploit it (C,D)."[39] Simply put, Prisoner's Dilemma suggests that, in discrete interactions, state preferences will prohibit cooperation.

Because players can learn conditional (tit-for-tat) reciprocity over time, however, repeated plays of the Prisoner's Dilemma game reveal the chance for cooperation. In "iterative" plays, actors can learn to reciprocate cooperative behavior so long as the other does not renege and the reciprocal act is immediate and matching.[40] Institutions help states see their long-run interest in cooperation and help enforce and maintain cooperative relations.[41]

Despite the valuable insights into cooperation through direct reciprocity provided by game theory, the approach has significant limits. Game theory leaves basic questions about the perceptions, beliefs, motives, and values of the actors involved outside the models.[42] Perhaps most significant, this approach *assumes* a set of fixed preferences, ignoring the events that shape or reshape those preferences. "The most important issue," Jervis explains, "may not be what happens after these [Prisoner's Dilemma] preferences have been established, but the preferences themselves. Much of the explanatory 'action' takes place in the formulation of preferences; we cannot afford to leave this topic offstage. . . . By taking preferences as given we beg what may be the most important question . . . when and why do decision makers see mutual cooperation as desirable?"[43]

Furthermore, the game theory approach tells us little about strategies of cooperation based on less immediate forms of reciprocal exchange. The focus in the literature tends toward the effects of immediate and matching exchanges of rewards and punishments, rather than more diffuse strategies. This approach undoubtedly derives from the psychological principles of learning on which game theory rests.[44]

This cursory review of international relations theory tells us that how a state weighs opportunities and constraints and calculates the choice of cooperation or noncooperation is a critically important issue. State preference formation and change, while integral to the issue of cooperation, are not adequately considered by game theory, or for that matter, by realist or liberal approaches. Both liberal and realist analyses turn on their view of states seeking their self-interest (defined in absolute and relative terms, respectively).[45] Both make powerfully reductionist, but operationally vague, assumptions about preferences that fail to address sufficiently the way states assess, reassess, and change their interests. For example, realists rightly note that states exercise power, often military power, in pursuit of their interests. Realists, however, by suggesting that power is both the means and the end of policy, do an inadequate job of explaining a state's interests and how the policies of other states or domestic factors act to change a state's definition of its interests.[46] Some liberals, in turn, too easily assume that states' interests mirror those of self-interested, value-maximizing individuals or societal groups, without considering interactive interstate processes that can inhibit cooperation.

Recent scholarship (including this book) takes a more agnostic position about the possibility of cooperation, thereby opening the door to a consideration of the factors that shape state interest toward or away from cooperation—such as incentives. Arthur Stein summarizes the problem aptly: "International relations involve both cooperation and conflict, evincing more cooperation than realists admit and more conflict than liberals recognize."[47] He concludes that the existence of cooperation or conflict depends on a state's payoff environment, its perceptions, its views on intertemporal trade-offs, and its strategic interactions with others.[48] Stein, too, returns to these questions: Under what conditions will a state be more likely to cooperate or to defect? What factors are important in shaping or reshaping a state's perceptions of its interest and its motivations?[49]

This book suggests that trade and technology incentives can, in some instances and in some measure, help explain the origin and evolution of state interest and behavior; therefore, generating hypotheses that seek to explain how incentives operate is a worthwhile endeavor. Hypothetically, trade and technology incentives can alter a state's calculation of self-interest by changing its perceptions, attitudes, perceived opportunities, and preferences. These changes could, in turn, alter the actions a state chooses to pursue. In short, economic incentives can affect a state's definition of its preferences by changing its external payoff environment *and* its domestic politics and, in some cases, alter its chosen policies. Chapter 2 of the book offers a set of logically related hypotheses on how incentives can foster cooperation.

Agent-level Explanations of Preferences

An often-cited shortcoming of international relations theories (and one contributing to the inadequate treatment of preferences) is the failure to integrate theoretical insights at the state level into their models. Helen Milner's essay on the status of interstate cooperation theory, for example, identifies the neglect of domestic politics as a weakness.[50] Not only does the prevailing realist and game-theoretic literature leave unattended questions of the formation of state preferences, it also makes unexamined assumptions about domestic politics, including "the strategies available to states to alter systemic conditions" and the "capacity of states to ratify and implement cooperative arrangements."[51] A better understanding of domestic politics would tell us how states arrive at their objectives and preferences and, in particular, how public and private sector actors reconcile interests.

To reach the issue of state preference formation and change, we must modify the assertions or assumptions about state preferences made by the previously described international relations theories. Several foreign policy decision-making theories help address the issue of state preference formation and behavior and are necessary to understand the operation of incentives.

Not all the approaches to explaining state preferences are important to this study. Four schools of thought at the national level or "agent level" are particularly useful in hypothesizing the role economic incentives play in formulating and changing state preferences. They include (1) statist/institutionalist approaches, (2) pluralism, (3) bureaucratic politics models, and (4) decision-making/cognition explanations.

Statist/institutionalist approaches hold that the strength and autonomy of the state matter most in determining preferences and behavior.[52] The state—an elite group of executive branch institutions and officials—steers foreign policy in accord with the dictates of the competitive environment of international relations.[53] These approaches focus on executive actors and institutions and their ability to shape foreign policy choices and behavior. The statist approach is not synonymous with the unitary, rational actor assumptions of some international relations theorists or the notion that bureaucracies and organizations are largely responsible for policy results. Rather, executive actors with goals and norms and certain enduring political institutions with established operating characteristics constitute the state.[54] These actors formulate policy in response to their internal goals and procedures and in response to the threats and opportunities provided by the international system.[55] The state's leaders and institutions possess a measure of autonomy from societal actors and the international system. National preferences flow from this interaction between the executive and its institutions as prompted by the international environment.

Statist approaches remind us that policy preferences and choices are not simply traceable to the interests of one or more groups, they are affected by structures.[56] The approach is compatible, therefore, with institutionalism. As Krasner argues, "Statist orientations place greater emphasis on institutional constraints, both formal and informal, on individual behavior."[57] In another work, he summarizes two basic reasons why institutions are essential to understanding preferences and policy choice: "First, capabilities and preferences, that is, the very nature of the actors, cannot be understood except as part of some larger institutional framework. Second, the possible options available at any given point in time are constrained by available institutional capabilities and these capabilities are themselves a product of some choices made during some earlier period."[58] Institutions, therefore, shape preferences and constrain activities.[59] Responses to external stimuli or societal forces are neither automatic nor costless.

In contrast, pluralism, a variant of liberal theory, views the political process within states (particularly the United States) as dominated by interest group activities. It suggests that state preference formation and state behavior are the result of bargaining and compromise among many voluntary, randomly arranged interest groups. The state, in this model, is seen as weak and often fragmented when competing with these groups and the coalitions they form.[60] Understanding the dispersion and fragmentation of authority among domestic groups and the process of forming a consensus is essential to understanding state preferences. Executive branch actors and institutions, which are the focus of statist theory, are seen by pluralists as merely aggregating and averaging the preferences and power of societal actors. Their state is not an autonomous actor with preferences and power in its own right. Leaders and state institutions are not sharply differentiated from their society. They are constrained, if not captured, by societal pressures.[61]

An organizational or bureaucratic politics model asserts that preferences and power of state bureaucracies shape national decisions and actions, often in ways that differ from the assumptions of rational actor models. Bureaucratic or organizational preferences are a combination of preexisting beliefs about national interests and a bureaucrat's personal interests, strongly colored by an interest in the continued health and welfare of the organization or bureau of which he or she is a part. Intranational games are important in shaping outcomes. Policies are fragmented, interpreted differently according to the established organizational missions of each bureaucracy, and emerge as a result of a political process. Bureaucracies tend to perpetuate exiting preferences or slow the process of adaptation to new environmental challenges.[62]

Finally, preferences can be identified with individual cognition and choice. The many theories at this level of analysis argue that actual decision making differs considerably from the assumptions of rationality.[63] One approach particularly important to the foreign policy of states is offered by Robert Jervis, who focuses on human cognition and its limitations. Jervis emphasizes the organizing beliefs of policymakers, or their "images," and the role these images play in their foreign policy choices. Important historic events shape these images, which are used later by policymakers to meet new situations.[64]

Preexisting images limit a leader's cognitive functions. As a result of trusting their images, decision makers act on established beliefs even in the face of new or contradictory information. Jervis notes that people resist cues that challenge their expectations and that once a policymaker commits to a course of action, negative feedback may have little impact on his or her decisions.[65] These conclusions are consistent with other psychological analyses of decision making.[66] State preferences, therefore, must be understood in the context of preexisting and enduring images held by decision makers; they are not merely rational responses to changing payoff environments or the product of organizational procedures.

Each of these agent-level theories holds important insights for an investigation into the operation of incentives. None holds the whole truth. The purpose of recounting them is not to endorse any one but to use them in the following chapter to create a framework for understanding the domestic political economy of incentives and to later use these "islands of theory" to generate hypotheses that, together with structural hypotheses, help us understand the operation of the independent variable—incentives.

The Case Studies and Case Study Methodology

As noted, this book examines three historical incentive cases. This comparative case study of three long-term incentive programs, while less parsimonious than some approaches, is a method that can help generate strong hypotheses and plausible statements of causality regarding how incentives work when many variables are involved. Keohane, for example, argues, "Any act of cooperation or apparent cooperation needs to be interpreted within the context of related actions, and of prevailing expectations and shared beliefs, before its meaning can be properly understood. Fragments of political behavior become comprehensible when viewed as part of a larger mosaic."[67] The case studies also constitute the empirical foundation for discerning general insights about the operation and effect of incentives for policymakers.

Each of the cases chosen for study was an important policy initiative. The case of the transfer of American civilian nuclear technology to Sweden was part of a dramatic departure in U.S. nuclear nonproliferation policy. Likewise, the U.S. decision to normalize economic relations with the PRC was among the most significant instances of long-term economic incentive programs in recent years. The opening of trade and technology exchange with Czechoslovakia was a major departure from the Cold War policy of economic containment of the East.

Moreover, each of these cases represents an instance of a long-term, diffuse attempt to influence and regularize behavior and cooperation. To isolate somewhat the impact of incentives, the cases selected involve cooperative interaction attempts occurring outside the context of shared regimes, that is, sets of rules, principles, norms, or decision-making procedures around which actors' expectations converge. Cooperative efforts in these cases did not occur within formal institutions to help regularize behavior and cooperation, to inhibit cheating (a factor important to reach cooperation under anarchy even for liberals), to sanction noncompliance, or to facilitate side payments between sender and recipient. Further, the states interacting in the U.S.-PRC case were of radically different political and economic systems in disparate ideological camps that did not have long-standing patterns of trust and cooperation. Czechoslovakia was isolated from the West for over forty years. Sweden, too, remained outside the East-West alliance structures of the period and possessed a strong tradition of looking after its own defense through its policy of armed neutrality or formal institutions. Thus, while numerous variables affected the outcome of the cases, the studies do control, to the degree permitted in international relations, some of the variables—regimes, institutions, and norms—that have been the foci of many studies of international cooperation and allow us to trace the process of incentives and cooperative influence.[68]

These are important cases for another reason as well. Each case presents a situation in which the sender is offering an economic and civilian technology package in implicit exchange for adjustments by the recipient in the area of "high politics" (political military-security relations) as opposed to adjustments in the "low politics" arena (economic or technological cooperation) alone. These are not cases in which the goal is merely state-to-state cooperation in peripheral areas that are relatively noncontentious, for example, a joint scientific undertaking or mutually rewarding economic exchange. Rather, these cases are programmatic incentives offered by the sender to foster policy adjustment in areas that go to matters directly related to the recipient's vital national interests. The cooperation sought is not a trivial, inconsequential, or secondary matter to either the sender or the recipient. Consequently, in these cases cooperation, to the extent it is found, is particularly important to international relations theorists and foreign policymakers.

Methodologically, these studies are "least likely" cases. That is, because of the absence of institutions, regimes, or normative consensus and given the area of desired cooperation, they present situations where prevailing theory suggests that cooperation through the use of an incentive strategy should fail. Although this book is more concerned with how incentives can produce cooperation rather than whether they can do so, the cases are potentially significant to those theoreticians interested in the possibility of interstate cooperation and those policymakers interested in the efficacy of incentives. It also suggests that incentives might operate in similar, if not stronger, fashion in multilateral institutionalized forums.

A word about the method for discerning the existence, nonexistence, or degree of cooperation in the case studies is required. Exploring the question of the relationship between an incentive program and cooperation requires a thorough understanding of actions and interactions and an estimation of the motives of two or more states—the sender(s) and the target(s). To locate patterns of cooperation or their absence, one must first identify the sender state's goals and the incentives it devises to achieve cooperative adjustment from the target state. Next, the target state's actions in the areas of interest to the sender before and after the receipt of the incentive (or promise thereof) must be analyzed to determine if the recipient's policies are adjusting along the lines desired by the sender state. If so, then the study must judge whether the apparent adjustment is in some measure other-regarding or merely reflects the recipient's pursuit of self-interest. That is, when the policies of the sender and the recipient coalesce, is it a case of harmony or is it cooperation? To answer this question, one must consider a state's motivation. Judging a recipient's motives contains a measure of subjectivity and is influenced by the observer's preexisting beliefs.[69] This study identifies discord, harmony, or cooperation based on an informed assessment of the recipient's actions gained by an empirical examination of the bilateral relationship during the incentive program and a synthesis of the expert interpretations of specialists and policymakers involved in the bilateral relationship. This historiographic method is no more, and may be less, subject to distortion than many statistical approaches.

Statistical approaches are not particularly useful for the goals of this study: hypotheses generation and policy recommendation. Statistical approaches may be more useful in a second stage of the research that attempts to "test" or evaluate the hypotheses.[70] Statistical approaches, while arguably more scientific, are problematic in searching for the outlines of a theory. That approach also lacks credibility to many policymakers as representative of the empirical reality in which they work. Furthermore, it is not certain that statistical approaches are more objective means of locating patterns of state interactions than historiographic means. Time series models based on the coding of events data can be a questionable portrayal of historical processes. This method does not overcome the problem of subjective determination of events as cooperative or noncooperative. Rather, it allows the theorist to run statistical tests with material that researchers classify earnestly, but subjectively, as cooperative or noncooperative based on subjective news reporting. Collecting and manipulating subjective data do not make the analysis more objective, only more abstract.

The counterfactual question also poses a methodological problem.[71] David Baldwin makes this point specifically about the exercise of economic policy instruments: "Power analysis always requires consideration of counterfactual conditions. If power relations involve some people getting other people to do something they otherwise would not do, the questions of what would have been done cannot be ignored."[72] He further explains that while the counterfactual problem cannot be ignored, neither can it easily be resolved. "The necessity of dealing with this question makes power analysis inherently messy, difficult, and frustrating. . . . Such discussions may amount to little more than educated guesses, but this is preferable to ignoring the problem."[73] The empirical work presented here will not ignore this question, nor can it fully resolve it. The method chosen to discern the existence or nonexistence of diffuse cooperation involves an in-depth and broad examination of the pattern of sender-recipient relations in the policy areas identified as those in which the sender seeks adjustments. If conducted carefully and thoroughly, the cases should generate a description of events that will support reasonable conclusions and hypotheses about the existence and extent of cooperation and the role of incentives on preference formation and behavior. As Alexander George has argued, this method can contribute to the further development of theory by identifying explanatory variables that influence the course of events.[74] The method is not offered as a test of these hypotheses, however.

Should the reader assume that my method too easily allows for a finding of cooperation, I would note that the indicator selected in this study helps correct for this problem. Incentives can influence a target state toward cooperative relations through changing its "beliefs, attitudes, opinions, expectations, emotions or propensities to act," in addition to changing its observable behavior.[75] By focusing on the changes in the behavior of the target state as the indicator of cooperation, this study has set up a stringent definition of *cooperation:* cooperation exists only when we can recognize it through a change in the target's policies. This approach tends to discount other forms of cooperative influence but is chosen because inferences about psychological constructs such as perceptions, emotions, beliefs, or motives are, as noted in the discussion of differentiating cooperation from harmony, highly problematic.[76]

CHAPTER 2

Toward a Theory of Economic Incentives

The goal of this chapter is to outline a logically consistent, two-level (structural/agent) explanation for how incentives can lead states to choose cooperation. As mentioned in chapter 1, the choice of interstate cooperation has embedded within it an internal choice or exchange of preferences by each party. These choices are interdependent, and both can be affected by trade and technology incentives.

The chapter begins by using the simplified international exchange model as a heuristic device to understand how a sender's economic incentives could alter the external environment of the recipient to produce a political concession or adjustment, that is, cooperation. This model is not sufficient in explaining how incentives produce cooperation, however. First, the simple exchange model does not capture the importance of technology to a state's welfare enhancement and hence technology's potential as a tool of political influence.[1] Second, by treating preference formation and change as exogenous factors, the simple exchange model fails to capture how incentives can affect actor-level choices in a cooperative direction over time. Thus, the goal of this chapter is to offer hypotheses about the effects of incentives on strategic interaction between states and domestic preference formation within them.

Changing the International Payoff Structure

An important exception to my generalization that scholars have ignored the power of trade is Albert O. Hirschman's work, *National Power and the Structure of Foreign Trade.* Hirschman tries to explain "why and how foreign trade might become or might consciously be used as an instrument of national power policy."[2] Although recognizing the potential for both positive and negative influence available through trade, Hirschman focuses on coercive influence, arguing that the power to interrupt commercial or financial relations with a country is a source of power that varies with the target's (1) net gain from the trade, (2) adjustment costs associated with the cutoff, and (3) vested interests in the trade.[3] The root cause of influence, then, is a country's dependence on trade.

R. Harrison Wagner's critique of Hirschman focuses on the assumption that asymmetrical economic relations *necessarily* translate into political influence. Wagner rejects that notion and asserts that influence cannot be conceptualized without a theory of bargaining and exchange.[4] Wagner's bargaining model helps us begin to see the operation of incentives at the structural level of international exchange.

Under his bargaining model, the use of trade for political influence requires that the exchange of economic resources for political concessions makes both parties to a relationship better off than they would be if they bargained over the distribution of the gains from the economic relationship alone.[5] The sender state can derive political influence from the recipient state's dependence on the gains from trade only if the sender is willing to sacrifice some of its gains from trade for the political concession. This trade-off requires that the sender place a greater monetary value on the political issue than the recipient does. Political influence, Wagner maintains, comes from paying part of one's gains from trade for a change in the recipient's political behavior, not from the mere existence of asymmetry. Influence is possible only "if a government that is attempting to exercise influence has a bargaining advantage with respect to the terms of trade that it has not exploited."[6] A graphical representation of this process is provided in the appendix to chapter 7.

Wagner's bargaining model allows us to see some important points about incentives operating at the level of international exchange (the strategic payoff environment). First, many situations arise where new gains from trade exist or where the terms of exchange could be made more favorable to a trading partner by a political act. The bargaining model helps us see that private exchange does not preclude the state from using trade and technology as a political instrument.

Second, we see that at the level of international exchange, economic incentives can shape state behavior much like sanctions do. Incentives alter a state's payoff environment by offering an exchange of economic gains from trade and technology transfer for political concessions. A decision by the sender to open mutually beneficial trade or grant the recipient state better terms of trade (relaxing a tariff, for example) is extended in exchange for a desired policy adjustment (political cooperation). In a sanction case, the sender is trying to collect a political concession for bargaining gains it has forgone earlier. With incentives, the sender is offering new or additional gains from trade and technology transfer for the concession.[7]

Wagner suggests that incentives should be less powerful instruments than sanctions because the recipient state necessarily values more highly the marginal unit of a good taken away (via sanctions) than an additional economic benefit of the same amount (via incentives). Because marginal utility for economic gain necessarily declines with each new unit of economic benefit, the sender's marginal influence derived from an incentive will be less than the influence of an equivalent amount of benefit taken away through a sanction. Wagner also claims that reallocation costs associated with the loss of existing trade are likely to be greater for the target than the reallocation costs associated with new trade or aid. For this reason also, economic sanctions should be a more influential policy instrument.

Wagner's analysis allows us to see some important points about incentives operating at the level of international exchange. Unfortunately, Wagner's conclusion that incentives are merely weak sanctions ignores many important differences between the two instruments, particularly the sources of incentives' strength and their potential for cooperative influence.

Under certain conditions, incentives may be compelling in altering the international environment facing states. For the reasons offered subsequently, several factors at the level of international exchange and domestic politics explain incentives' fuller potential for cooperative influence. First, although a recipient necessarily has a declining *marginal* utility for an incentive, what may be more important is the recipient's *total* utility for the goods or technology. If total utility remains substantially positive during the influence attempt, the incentive could represent a powerful inducement. In the cases that follow, the recipients valued the commodities and technologies offered because they were important to the recipients' economic and political goals, scarce in the recipient states, and the terms offered by the sender for obtaining them were, relative to past experience, quite favorable.

Strong total utility is more likely when advanced technology is part of the package, as technology is integral to a state's overall production capability. A simple gains from trade model fails to capture fully the dynamic role of technology in production and hence its long-run potential as a political incentive. The importance of technology is better captured by considering its role in the recipient's production process. For economists, a society's ability to produce a given level of output from existing factor inputs is dependent on the state of technology.[8] The law of diminishing returns to productive inputs can be offset by technological innovation, and economists have estimated that technology plays the dominant role in increasing productivity.[9] Robert Solow's work on the American economy, for example, estimated that more than half the historic increase in U.S. productivity was attributable to technological change.[10] That technology, a factor so critical to national welfare, might be a powerful tool of positive political influence seems obvious, yet it is not appreciated by international relations theory,[11] nor is it fully captured in a bargaining and exchange model.

The importance of technology as an incentive is illustrated in the U.S.-PRC case. Chapter 4 discusses the emergence of a new policy line in China in the early 1970s that moved away from self-reliance toward greater importation of foreign goods and technology to speed China's development and modernization. China's technological isolation during the 1950s and 1960s left it far behind the West as the Soviet and Eastern European technology base transferred to China in the mid-1950s decayed. Thus, by 1978 the Chinese Communist party had officially endorsed the "Four Modernizations" plan to revitalize the Chinese economy in agriculture, industry, national defense, and science and technology by the year 2000, and the party had committed itself to the goal of China's modernization through the adoption of Western technology and integration into the world economy.

The United States, meanwhile, was reassessing China's strategic importance and economic needs and fashioned an economic incentive policy that promised China access to Western capital and technology and access to the U.S. market in exchange for greater political and security cooperation. Essential elements of the package included most favored nation (MFN) tariff treatment, relaxation on high technology export controls governing U.S. and Western technology transfers to China, and access to Western private and public capital markets. The impact of these incentives on Chinese foreign policy in the early and mid-1980s is discussed in chapter 4.

Second, Wagner's analysis also fails to consider the difference between sanctions and incentives with regard to the costs borne by the sender state. Incentives, unlike sanctions, to the extent they open up new opportunities for trade and exchange (relaxing an embargo, for example), create opportunities for both sender and recipient to garner a portion of the new gains from trade—an improvement in economic utility for both. The bargaining model requires that the sender not fully exploit its market power over the terms of trade but allow the recipient to gather economic benefit from new trade or to refrain from fully exploiting its market power over existing trade to gain political concessions from the recipient. By creating new gains from trade or forgoing some of its potential gains from existing trade, the sender acquires the means for bargaining for political concessions. This point should not obscure the fact that *both* sender and recipient can gain economically from the creation of new trade, and both share in varying degrees from existing trade. A sender can use an incentive policy both to change the payoff structure of the recipient to influence its political decisions *and* to increase its own absolute gains from trade in some instances. Other incentives involving ongoing trade may require a distributional change between sender and recipient in relative shares of gains from trade, but in the cases that follow, the gain-creating benefits of incentives accrue to both sender and recipient. This observation suggests that incentives should give the sender greater interest in maintaining the policy and that incentives are less likely to collapse under their own weight. It also differentiates trade and technology transfer incentives, which can create new economic gains for both parties, from foreign aid.[12] Foreign aid programs, like sanctions, are costly to the sender state. Simply put, incentives can be a win-win instrument, whereas sanctions are a lose-lose instrument, whose effectiveness depends on which party is better able to withstand the attendant costs. This difference carries important implications for the domestic political effects of incentives discussed subsequently.

Finally, in those instances when the sender possesses market power in the incentive, the impact is enhanced because market power creates a larger potential benefit to exchange for the desired political concession. Unlike economic sanctions, however, market power is not a strict necessity. In the case studies that follow, the sender had substantial market power in the incentive goods.

The international exchange model, like much economic and international relations theory, assumes a set of fixed preferences and is an incomplete conceptualization.[13] This study suggests that much of the explanation for how incentives work lies outside the bargaining model, which makes unitary rational actor assumptions and does not incorporate domestic factors accounting for changes in state preferences.

To understand the process of state preference change, the analysis must penetrate the state and look inside to the domestic politics of the sender and the recipient and the formulation of their policy preferences.[14] An *internal* choice or exchange occurs in both the sender and the recipient state as well as an external exchange between them. Before an international exchange of economic benefits for political concessions can occur, a sender state must change its preference for political concessions versus economic gains to alter the terms of trade,[15] and a recipient state must adopt an internal exchange function favoring gains from trade (and political concessions) rather than political autonomy.

Why would state preferences shift in the sender state and how do recipient state preferences come to accept a proffered incentive? Answers to these questions require incorporating insights from the theories of agent-level preference formation—statism, institutionalism, pluralism, and decision-maker cognition—noted in chapter 1.[16]

This study hypothesizes that sanctions and incentives may operate in substantially different ways at the level of national preference formation. I will address several ways that, in contrast to sanctions, the power of economic incentives is enhanced or less likely to be diminished by its domestic operation.

Sender Preferences

In the cases investigated, the sender's initial decision to launch an economic incentive program was fundamentally consistent with statist explanations of executive actors seizing new opportunities offered by the international environment. In this sense, little difference may exist between incentive policy-making and sanction policy-making. For example, President Nixon startled the world with the revelation that the United States was normalizing relations with China. Similarly, a few executive actors and institutions in the Carter White House made the decision to "tilt" toward China (and away from the Soviet Union) in economic and technological relations following the Soviet Union's invasion of Afghanistan.[17] In the latter instance, the state demonstrated substantial policy autonomy in responding to changes in the external environment. Other branches of government and societal actors were not the moving forces behind these policies. Likewise, Eisenhower's decision to use American civilian nuclear technology as a positive instrument of U.S. foreign policy was a uniquely presidential policy, with input from a few members of the Atomic Energy Commission (itself a collection of executive branch expert advisers). Domestic interests, in the form of a civilian nuclear power industry, were largely created by the state. The offer of U.S. trade and technology benefits to Czechoslovakia for cooperation in nonproliferation came largely from the Bush White House, although allied powers and U.S. exporters had agitated for a more liberal American technology transfer and trade policy before the move.

By initiating bold new policies, state actors often command strong support. Public opinion, in these incentives episodes, initially followed the lead of elites. One should recall the general relief and euphoria that surrounded Eisenhower's "Atoms for Peace" address to the United Nations in the 1950s or the U.S. decision to recognize China and normalize relations in the 1970s. Incentives, which the public views as pacific and consistent with American generosity and belief in open markets, rarely raise public fears. This acceptance is particularly true of trade and technology transfer as opposed to foreign aid, which traditionally has had uneven domestic support.

An incentive policy or sanctions policy involves more than the decision to launch such a program and its promulgation, however. As time passed, societal actors took a larger role in the direction of the policy, and incentives began to operate differently than sanctions in the sender state. In subsequent time periods, the insights of approaches—like pluralism—that focus on societal interests became increasingly relevant.

Many of those who have studied sanctions conclude that the implementation of a sanction policy in the sender state invariably implicates societal actors and creates conflicts between the state and society. Otto Wolff von Amerongen asserts, "As a rule, an embargo will affect a country's exports, it is a limitation of export. It should therefore be considered normal when in connection with such decisions, a conflict between the interest of a government and the interest of economic bodies becomes apparent."[18] Likewise the study of economic sanctions by Gary Hufbauer, Jeffrey Schott, and Kimberley Elliott concludes that, with regard to societal groups in the sender state, "Business firms at home may experience severe losses when sanctions interrupt trade and financial contacts. . . . After the first flush of patriotic enthusiasm, such complaints can undermine a sanction initiative."[19] As for the larger public, they assert, "Even though popular opinion in the sender country may welcome the introduction of sanctions, public support often dissipates over time."[20]

In contrast, the cases that follow suggest that incentives are more likely to maintain or increase their base of support in the sender state over time. Unlike sanctions, support for trade and technology incentives spreads as exporters and investors take a growing interest in the gains from trade and technology transfer associated with new or expanded commercial relations.

In the case of the offer of civilian nuclear technology in chapter 3, the beneficiaries included the emerging American civilian light-water nuclear plant industry (General Electric and Westinghouse, in particular). High and medium technology exporters of all types benefited from improving commercial relations with China.[21] In opening trade and technology transfer to Eastern Europe, telecommunications and information technologies exporters acquired new markets.

It is true that import-competing producers in the sender state might oppose an incentive policy because of the economic adjustment costs it imposes on them. A case in point would be American textile industries adversely impacted by expanded trade with the PRC. Although adjustment costs pose a domestic obstacle to some trade incentive policies, it is not an insurmountable problem. States regularly incur the costs of domestic adjustment for overall welfare gains from expanded trade. Indeed, the history of international trade liberalization during the past fifty years attests to the willingness of states to make this trade-off. In the case of trade incentive policies, the sender state often anticipates gaining both politically and economically from the new relationship with the recipient state. The potential political and economic gains for the sender state should make it more willing to shoulder any domestic adjustment costs attending its policies.

In short, many forms of trade and technology transfer incentives, unlike sanctions, do not create fundamental state-society antagonism. Trade and technology incentives, as policies that often create economic gains for the sender as well as the recipient, can gather political support over time. In fact, after the initial establishment of incentive programs, societal interests in maintaining incentives may limit state flexibility in rescinding benefits. The American difficulty in making a credible threat to China over the possible withdrawal of its MFN status is an example. In sum, one part of the explanation for how incentives work is the hypotheses that incentives, in contrast to sanctions, do not necessarily create a state-society antagonism in the sender nation, and, in some cases, the interests of the sender state and its societal groups that are strongly affected by the policy may reinforce the incentive.

As to orchestrating broader domestic support, incentives may be an easier policy instrument to rally a winning domestic coalition behind the other economic instruments. Because incentives have an overtly political purpose (unlike, say, a GATT-mandated tariff reduction), policymakers can more credibly invoke ideals such as global peace or national security (in addition to economic benefit for the domestic sectors) to garner support for the incentive strategy.

Incentives, unlike more bellicose measures such as sanctions, raise few fears or concerns in the sender state's populace and, indeed, are generally good for domestic propaganda purposes. President Eisenhower's Atoms for Peace initiative, directed at Sweden, among others, was particularly ingenious in this respect. That incentive strategy allowed the president to transcend his advisers' recommendations for greater candor with the American people about the potential (good and evil) of the atom and give concrete meaning to a positive vision of using new knowledge and technology to build greater world peace and prosperity. Similarly, the reopening to China was a propaganda plus for American policymakers, resonating with the public's desire to see a relaxation in Cold War tensions and widespread (but naive) belief that the United States had reestablished its special relationship with China dating back to the Open Door era.

This assertion does not imply that domestic interests will uniformly endorse incentives. Every major policy departure has its legitimate critics and those looking for partisan advantage. Because of their noncoercive character, incentive policies are particularly vulnerable to attack as "weak" responses or as "appeasement." Recent criticism of U.S. incentive policies toward North Korea provide an example. Policymakers may need to take such warning seriously because, as discussed in a later chapter, inappropriately applied or executed incentives can lead to appeasement of aggression. On the other hand, precisely because incentives are not overtly coercive measures, they do not raise the same fears of conflict escalation in the general public as economic sanctions or military policies do. The cases examined suggest that the possibility of escalating hostilities alarms the public and is more likely to raise reservations than the possibility of appeasement does.

Recipient Preferences

Incentives also operate differently than sanctions in the domestic politics of the recipient state. The sanctions literature repeatedly asserts that domestic antidotes generated in the recipient state limit the power of economic sanctions. The two domestic antidotes most often cited are the tendency of economic sanctions to (1) unify the target country in support of the government and in resistance to an external threat and (2) compel the target country to search for commercial alternatives.[22] Both reactions move the target country away from a preference for the sender's desired political concessions.

The first antidote, the "rally-around-the-flag" effect, has two dimensions—political and economic. Politically, because sanctions are a threat to harm the target state, its leaders can marshal popular support and suppress societal dissent by an appeal to national pride or survival to oppose sanctions. Fidel Castro's and Saddam Hussein's ability to gather support for resistance to foreign pressure provide two vivid examples.[23] The "rally-around-the-flag" effect tends to strengthen the preference of the recipient state for political autonomy as opposed to political compromise and adjustment consistent with the sender's wishes.

Economically, a sanction, by raising the domestic price of the sanctioned import, will cause the target government to intervene extensively in the market to organize trade in that sector as a monopsonist and capture some of the economic rents generated by the sanctions.[24] The target government then can use the difference between domestic and world prices to ration the goods as a political resource and consolidate its ruling coalition by offering access to the sanctioned good to preferred domestic groups in return for political resistance to the sanctions.

The work of David Rowe helps us see that, in addition to strengthening the material resources of the target state, sanctions create societal actors in the target country with a stake in ensuring that the sanctions continue. Sanctions create winners and losers in the target nation. He explains:

> Sanctions on the target country's imports generate a transfer of surplus from domestic consumers of the imported good to import-competing producers. Because import-competing producers will capture this windfall as long as the sanctions persist, this group has a strong economic incentive to encourage the target government to reject the demands of the sanctioning countries.[25]

Because beneficiaries of the sanctions typically are more concentrated than those harmed (consumers), we might expect this group to exercise greater political influence. For political and economic reasons, therefore, sanctions encourage the target state to form or maintain preferences rejecting the sender's demands.[26]

Incentives are less likely to produce this antidote. Instead, the case studies suggest they can penetrate the recipient state and bolster those state or societal actors in the recipient state who are most sympathetic, or least resistant, to the political concessions the sender desires. Because they are noncoercive instruments that provide a tangible material benefit that some recipient actor can appropriate (as well as nontangible benefits such as recognition or legitimacy), incentives find natural allies in the recipient state that reinforce the sender's message and influence. Arguably, overreaching or overbearing incentives could antagonize the recipient rather than encourage cooperation. The point remains, however, that unlike sanctions, incentives do not necessarily challenge the sovereignty of the recipient state.

Because they are not, per se, an affront to recipient state sovereignty, incentives are more likely to penetrate the state and shape the process of preference formation within the recipient state's society. Within the political economy of the recipient state, incentives encourage those state or societal actors who have the most to gain economically to be more sympathetic or less resistant to the political concessions the sender seeks. Regarding technology transfer to Sweden, for example, the internal ally was Sweden's emerging civilian nuclear power industry, which was eager for American light water technology and material and unconcerned about the nonproliferation commitments that acceptance of the technology entailed. Within the Swedish government, American incentives resonated with the antibomb factions of the ruling Social Democratic party and became a device for certain bureaus (e.g., the air force) that opposed the use of defense resources for the creation of nuclear bombs.[27] In China, the economic and modernization benefits derived from cooperation with the West strengthened the hand of Deng Xiaoping and the reformers at a critical juncture in China's foreign policy. In the Czech case, the economic benefits not only offered new technology and material rewards to emerging private-sector actors, but also strengthened the legitimacy of new leaders, such as Vaclav Havel, who had committed themselves to reintegration with the West. Each of these allies assisted the sender in moving the recipient toward cooperative adjustment.

A qualification to this point should be noted, however. Analogous to the possibility of import-competing producers' opposition to incentives in the sender state, incentives also can create opposition among import-competing producers in the recipient state. The case of U.S. and Western economic incentives to Czechoslovakia in exchange for cooperation in technology transfer controls and arms transfer restraint illustrates the point. In that instance, recipient cooperation was complicated because the costs of arms export restraints fell heavily on munitions manufacturers concentrated in Slovak regions. Chapter 5 discusses this struggle among state and contending societal interests in depth. Nonetheless, although societal groups in the recipient state actually or potentially hurt by an incentive policy may raise objections, such incentives necessarily create potential partners in the recipient state who benefit economically and are motivated to see incentives work. While the outcome of contending domestic interests is never certain, incentives create a clear possibility that a recipient interest group with a potential stake in the gains from trade will join the sender in urging cooperative adjustment.

The second cited antidote to sanctions is the tendency to drive the target into a search for alternative suppliers who are encouraged to supply the target because the politically created scarcity resulting from an embargo offers them unique economic opportunities. The power of sanctions can be "broken" if the target can locate an alternative source of supply for the embargoed good(s). Lisa Martin argues, "Although the goals of sanctions are highly political, states' ability to use sanctions is subject to the rule of economic exchange. This means that unilateral sanctions, those undertaken by just one government, usually fail because the target can find alternative markets or suppliers for the sanctioned good."[28]

In contrast, this study hypothesizes that the offer of an economic incentive providing new gains from trade does not create a strong desire in the recipient to undermine the offer by seeking an alternative supplier. Furthermore, incentives do not create economic conditions that encourage new entrants or third-party suppliers to offset the sender's efforts. When an incentive is offered, the recipient simply can choose to reject it and maintain its political autonomy, leaving it no worse off than before. Third-party suppliers are important in incentive cases to the extent a potential recipient could "shop" the incentive offered from one potential sender for better terms from another potential sender. The ability of small states to entice the United States and the former Soviet Union into a bidding war for political influence during the Cold War would be a case in point. In this sense, a third-party supplier could offset the potential influence of an offered incentive, but the motivation to intervene would be political, not economic. Third-party involvement would require conditions where two or more competing states each sought similar political goals and each was willing to use economic incentives to secure them. As a general matter, however, it is unlikely that a potential recipient state could "break" an incentive by seeking a third-party supplier. The Cold War case is likely an exceptional one.

Moreover, it is unlikely that a potential recipient would even try to "break" an incentive. As "prospect theory" argues, states concern themselves with the potential of loss far more than the possibility of additional gain. Prospect theory—an alternative to rational choice/expected utility analysis—as applied to international relations suggests that states prefer the status quo and "seem to make greater efforts to preserve the status quo against a threatened loss than to improve their position by a comparable amount."[29] Thus, unlike sanctions, whose threatened economic and reputational loss motivate and mobilize the recipient to search for third-party suppliers, incentives do not compel a potential recipient to pursue a better offer. As to third-party suppliers, politically created scarcity precipitated by sanctions induces the entry of new suppliers. The offer of new supply on more favorable terms by a sender has the opposite effect. The Swedish case study illustrates these points. America's incentive strategy shaped Sweden's decision-making environment for more than a decade without inviting third-party interference.

Decision-maker Cognition and Misperception

Incentives may operate differently than coercive instruments at the decision-making level as well. Scholars who have examined decision-maker cognition and choice as a source of national preferences tell us that once committed to a course of action, decision makers often use established images to filter information to resist negative feedback. Likewise, the work of Irving Janis and Leon Mann suggests that warnings, threats, and the possibility of loss will often lead decision makers to be insensitive to information critical of their policies—a pattern of defensive avoidance.[30]

These insights and the cases suggest that sanctions are more likely than incentives to engender or aggravate misperception or produce these cognitive pathologies. Sanctions, therefore, may impede cooperation where incentives encourage it.[31] Incentives, a noncoercive influence attempt, do not threaten a decision maker in the recipient country with loss (both tangible loss of existing gains from trade and loss of reputation at home). Unlike sanctions' punishment or opprobrium, incentives should be less likely to produce defensive, rigid, or obstinate reactions that impede clear communication and policy adjustment between countries over the long term. In fact, the following cases suggest that incentives can open new channels of communication, encourage further negotiations, reduce the hostility and fear that may have characterized the bilateral relationship, and permit the recipient greater freedom to react cooperatively without fear of economic or reputational loss. Ironically, the ability of the recipient to characterize its policy adjustment in response to an incentive as self-motivated (rather than coerced) may be an important strength of incentives as a policy instrument and yet one of the reasons it is easy to overlook or underestimate their effects. The China case illustrates this point best as incentives in the economic and technology sphere helped dissolve decades of mistrust and mutual hostility.

Further, incentives, by highlighting the desired policy adaptation sought in the recipient, rather than singling out an undesired direction in another state's policies, may convey more precise and constructive information than sanctions. Incentives show the sender's desired or preferred course of adjustment rather than sanctioning an existing or anticipated policy. In this respect, incentives may perform the information-providing function of regimes in developing cooperation.[32] Punishment does not, in itself, communicate the sender's desired response; it merely points out one of the many undesired responses. Punishments have value in indicating the sender's displeasure, blocking the actions of the target, or satisfying the sender's desire for justice or revenge, but they are less than ideal for communicating the desire or direction for long-term cooperation.[33] In fact, they can quickly lead to communication gridlock. For example, in describing the long embargo period in U.S.-PRC relations that preceded the decision to offer economic incentives, John Raser notes, "The persistent pattern of communication between these powers consists of punishment, threats, condemnation, and frustration of drive reduction. The position of both is one of boycott, verbal hostility in the world forum, and military deployment at the highest state of readiness. There is little or no attempt to tell the other of ways in which they might behave which would meet their own needs and still be acceptable."[34] Simply put, if long-run cooperation, rather than punishment or demonstration of displeasure, is the goal, then incentives communicate better than sanctions. In many cases, but not all, clearer communication can facilitate cooperation.[35]

For example, in moving away from trade and technology denial and toward expanded commercial contact with reform-minded countries of Central Europe like Czechoslovakia, the United States communicated clearly and specifically its desired quid pro quo—the establishment of internal nonproliferation technology control institutions—and worked closely with these countries in realizing this objective. In contrast, the Cold War policy of trade and technology denial, while serving the goal of containment by imposing costs on a military and political rival, did little to communicate a preference or path for cooperation.

Conclusion

This chapter moves toward a two-level exchange theory of economic incentives. First, it explains how incentives can change a state's payoff environment to create the possibility for an exchange of economic benefits for political concessions. Second, it looks at the adoption of preferences that occurs within the sender and recipient states and hypothesizes how incentives might operate at that level in producing cooperation. Rather than reiterate the call for an integrated structural/agent, international/ domestic explanation, it seeks to provide one that is logically consistent. The interactive international and domestic impacts of incentives must be considered together in developing a sound explanation.

At the international system level, trade and technology incentives can shape state behavior in ways similar, but not identical, to sanctions and aid. Incentives alter the payoff environment of states by offering an exchange of economic gains from trade and technology transfer for political concessions. This study suggests that under certain conditions, incentives may be compelling in altering state behavior and fostering bilateral cooperation over time. They work better when (1) the recipient's marginal utility for the goods or gains from trade remains substantially positive (that is, total utility is increasing), which may be likely in instances where advanced technology is part of the package, (2) both the sender and the recipient stand to gain in economic terms through the creation of new trade, and (3) the sender possesses market power in the incentive goods. Still, considered only at the international level, incentives could be hastily dismissed as weak instruments for fostering cooperation. The theoretical prediction of limited efficacy does not fit well with my empirical findings and recommends an investigation of agent-level factors.

Incentives also affect the domestic political economy of agents (states) by shaping preferences in the sender and recipient in a manner that enhances or is less likely to impede cooperation. This affect is interdependent with the structural affect (changing the payoff environment), and an appreciation of both is necessary to understand how incentives might foster bilateral cooperation.[36] At the agent level, the argument draws on several approaches set out in chapter 1 to understand state preference formation and change. It highlights four ways in which the power of economic incentives may be undiminished or enhanced by its operation in the domestic societies of the sender and the recipient, in contrast to sanctions. First, societal actors in the sender state who stand to gain economically from expanded trade lend support for an incentive over time, thereby improving the policy's legitimacy and endurance. Public opinion in the sender state is unlikely to oppose an incentive. Second, certain actors in the recipient state who can appropriate the economic benefits tend to ally with the sender state and reinforce its efforts to move the recipient's policy preference in the direction of the sender's intent. Third, incentives are unlikely to create an impetus to elude or undermine its influence through the search for third-party suppliers or create the economic conditions that invite new entrants. Finally, incentives convey more precise information to decision makers in the recipient state in a manner that is less likely to be filtered, avoided, or resisted by them.

The case studies that follow illustrate many of these hypotheses. They allow us to trace the role of trade and technology incentives as one of many variables in influencing bilateral relations. The cases also provide an empirical base for discerning general insights about the operation and effect of incentives for policymakers in chapter 6.

CHAPTER 3

Civilian Nuclear Technology Incentives and U.S. Nuclear Nonproliferation Policy: The Case of Sweden

The United States has opposed the spread of nuclear weapons to other countries since the onset of the nuclear age. During the post–World War II period, American policymakers and the American public came to see the proliferation of nuclear weapons as a threat to U.S. security.[1] President Kennedy warned of this danger in a statement that could have been delivered by any of his predecessors or successors when he said, "I ask you to stop and think for a moment what it would mean to have nuclear weapons in so many hands, in the hands of countries large and small, stable and unstable, responsible and irresponsible, scattered throughout the world."[2]

While the norm of nonproliferation rarely generated dissent in any sector of the policy-making community, the means to this end has been a continual source of political controversy. From the 1940s through the 1960s the United States pursued several divergent approaches toward nonproliferation. Those that have examined the course of U.S. nonproliferation policy often divide its early history into three distinct phases: (1) beginning with the wartime experience, an era of secrecy and efforts to promote multilateral control of all atomic energy; (2) a phase of active promotion of the peaceful use of atomic energy under safeguards beginning with President Eisenhower's "Atoms for Peace" address of 1953 and a relaxation of secrecy restraints permitting the development of a domestic power industry; and (3) a program that emphasized the role of an international regime for controlling the spread of nuclear weapons while promoting the peaceful application of nuclear technology embodied in the Nonproliferation Treaty of 1968 and an expanded safeguard role for the International Atomic Energy Agency.[3] This study will focus on the second stage of U.S. nonproliferation policy, with particular attention to the United States's affirmative use of the peaceful atom as a tool of its nonproliferation policy.

Changing the External Environment to
Induce Cooperation

In a bold address to the United Nations General Assembly in 1953, President Eisenhower, in a speech entitled "Atomic Power for Peace," charted a new course toward the goal of nonproliferation. The approach reflected Eisenhower's belief that conditions called for the United States to move beyond mere candor with the American public about the negative capabilities of atomic weapons to a program that would accentuate the peaceful, commercial potential of the atom. Eisenhower was aware that the existing program of nuclear secrecy not only deluded the American people, but it also had failed to prevent the steady dispersion of nuclear weapons and nuclear power capabilities internationally. An international understanding was necessary to constrain and direct the spread of technology. Eisenhower would offer an American plan for making available the fruits of peaceful nuclear technology in exchange for agreements that would slow the spread of nuclear weapons.

Eisenhower proposed that those nations with nuclear capabilities contribute natural uranium and fissionable material to an international stockpile that would be regulated by an International Atomic Energy Agency under the jurisdiction of the United Nations. The agency would manage the stockpile and allocate it for peaceful purposes, especially electrical energy production, while ensuring that recipients did not divert these distributions to military purposes. Unlike earlier American proposals, Eisenhower's plan did not call for international ownership and management of sensitive activities. Rather, it envisioned national programs under international safeguards,[4] that is, a system of inspection and monitoring that could alert the world community to any diversion of atomic material or technology to a military purpose in the hope of deterring such violations.[5] The Eisenhower speech did not provide specifics on how to carry out his proposal, however.

The speech marked a fundamental change in the U.S. approach to nonproliferation policy. Abandoning the assumptions of the policy of secrecy, Eisenhower proposed, as the name of the speech implies, a tradeoff: American nuclear material and expertise that allowed others to develop peaceful applications of atomic power in exchange for pledges from recipients not to use the transferred technology for military purposes and for permission to conduct some form of international inspection. James Schlesinger, a notable observer of the address, reflected on "Eisenhower's grand leap of faith." "Atoms for Peace," as the speech would soon be known, contained a simple quid pro quo: "If we are to preserve a world in which other countries voluntarily refrain from seeking nuclear weapons, they must be given incentives to do so."[6] Eisenhower's plan offered an affirmative use of peaceful American nuclear technology as a means of limiting the proliferation of nuclear weapons. While denial of all technology and materials might be preferable in the abstract, technological and political reality meant that "cooperation in civilian nuclear programs would be preferable to independent national developments with no constraint as to military applications."[7] Other nations could be discouraged from building their own uranium processing plants, preventing the spread of fissionable material and, thus, weapons capabilities.[8] In exchange, the United States would remove the barriers of atomic isolation and allow the circulation of civilian technical information and nuclear material under international control.

The new American policy was meant to serve several goals, some which complemented each other, some which were largely illusory.[9] One clear motivation of the new policy was to prevent the further proliferation of nuclear weapons technology and civilian technology that, left unregulated, could be freely diverted to military purposes at a nation's discretion. Eisenhower in 1953 warned of the dangers of proliferation wherein "the dread secret . . . now possessed by several nations will eventually be shared by others—possibly all others."[10] The spread of nuclear weapons undermined U.S. security because the country's substantial deterrent capability was deemed less effective against a surprise attack. It became the goal of U.S. policy to "erect an international web of technical dependency relationships that would allow them to control the domestic nuclear development of other nations."[11] In addition, the "Atoms for Peace" proposal could slow the growth of nuclear arsenals and expand the United States's political influence and, eventually, commercial opportunities.

Although certain elements of Eisenhower's vision were never realized—for example, the planned stockpiling of nuclear materials—the proposal led to a reversal in U.S. secrecy strategy embodied in the Atomic Energy Act of 1946 (AEA).[12] In February 1954, President Eisenhower sent a message to Congress encouraging them to translate his "Atoms for Peace" proposal into legislation. The president noted that the statutory restrictions of the 1946 AEA, based on the American monopoly of atomic weapons and limited applications of nuclear technology in civilian fields, were "inconsistent with the realities of 1954." Eisenhower concluded that these restrictions impeded America's exploitation of nuclear energy for the benefit of its people and those of friendly nations.[13] He recommended that amendments to the 1946 legislation provide: (1) broader cooperation with U.S. allies in certain atomic energy matters, (2) improved procedures for the control and dissemination of atomic energy information, and (3) encouragement of wide participation in the development of peacetime uses of atomic energy in the United States.[14]

Congress gave concrete meaning to Eisenhower's vision in the 1954 revision of the AEA. The new legislation removed most controls on the classification of nuclear research information, approved private ownership of nuclear facilities and fissionable material, authorized the government to enter into agreements for cooperation with other nations on the peaceful use of nuclear energy that would permit the transmission of information and certain nuclear materials abroad,[15] and laid the groundwork for the establishment of an international atomic energy agency.[16] By 1954, the president and Congress had concluded that the end of the American nuclear monopoly, British success in the early development of atomic reactors, and France's independent nuclear program had seriously challenged the U.S. policy of nuclear secrecy and denial. If the Soviet Union possessed nuclear capabilities, it made little sense for the United States to deny nuclear information, technology, and material to its allies. Failure to share atomic technology in a positive way could cost the United States greatly in prestige and influence during a period of intense Cold War rivalry. Secrecy was harmful at home as well, fueling public fears of the destructive power of this new technology and wasting the U.S. competitive advantage in a potentially important commercial technology by inhibiting the freedom of scientists and engineers.

Beginning in 1955, the United States adopted a policy of technology exchange through a series of bilateral Agreements for Cooperation with several nations that transferred nuclear research and power reactors, enriched uranium, and training in exchange for the recipient's assurances that it would not divert the technology and materials to military purposes—that is, building atomic bombs—and guarantees that the United States could exercise certain forms of safeguards to verify the material's disposition.

Recognizing both the inevitable spread of nuclear technology and the virtual American monopoly over certain nuclear technologies and enriched uranium, the United States hoped to shape the desires and direction of countries like Sweden away from developing weapons capability based on natural uranium and technology outside American controls and safeguards.[17] On January 18, 1956, an Agreement for Cooperation with Sweden took effect.[18]

Appreciating the nonproliferation effect of the U.S. incentive strategy requires a basic understanding of reactor technologies. Essentially two types of civilian nuclear technologies were available during the 1950s and 1960s. Both produced plutonium (a weapons material) as a by-product, but from the standpoint of proliferation, they presented very different implications. One method, the approach originally favored by Sweden, relied on "natural" uranium. Reactors can use natural uranium as fuel with heavy water (D_2O) to generate energy. A heavy water reactor (HWR) "burns," or fissions, a portion of its radioactive uranium (U-235) and converts another portion of its inert uranium (U-238) into the element plutonium (Pu-239). Technicians can reprocess plutonium from the spent fuel to make a nuclear weapon core.

Because natural uranium was available from several sources outside U.S. control, the HWR approach presented proliferation problems from an American perspective. A country with a viable HWR program using non-American fuel would have an independent supply of plutonium for the manufacture of nuclear bombs.

In contrast, the American approach used "enriched uranium" fuel (that is, with a higher concentration of U-235) and "light water" reactors (LWRs) with H_2O as moderator in creating nuclear energy. During the 1950s and 1960s, the United States had a free world monopoly on enriched uranium and enrichment capabilities, that is, market power in the incentive goods. Enriched uranium, once created, could release vastly greater quantities of energy than natural uranium.

By encouraging countries to rely on enriched uranium and LWRs for their energy needs, the United States could inhibit weapons proliferation. Under the agreements for cooperation, the United States made generous offers to sell or lease enriched uranium to friendly nations for exclusively peaceful purposes. The United States also offered technology along with the safeguarded fuel: first research reactors and later commercially viable electricity reactors. Furthermore, the U.S. Atomic Energy Commission (AEC) priced the enriched uranium fuel so low compared to the cost of developing independent enrichment capabilities that the American offer created a powerful economic rationale for Western European nations to forgo development of uranium enrichment plants. Indeed, a secret 1954 U.S. State Department memo recommended this strategy for Sweden and other potential nuclear states in Europe:

> There are constant indications that France as well as other Northern European countries such as Sweden are considering the construction of plants for the production of slightly enriched uranium. If we were to make such material available it could undoubtedly be done in such a way as to achieve the delaying of such construction. A study should in any case be done as to whether it is in the interest of American security to have such enrichment plants operating. Should the answer turn out to be negative it would still be possible at this early stage to pre-

vent it, but the price for doing so would probably lie in a quid pro quo involving enriched materials.[19]

In short, U.S. foreign policy came to accept that the spread of nuclear technology was inevitable and "it was wise to seek to control that which could not be prevented. Atoms for Peace was designed to spread American controls internationally by means of spreading American nuclear technology and hardware."[20]

Equally important to the bilateral agreements in serving the nonproliferation strategy, the passage of the Atomic Energy Act of 1954 opened the door for the creation of a civilian nuclear energy industry. Domestically, the new legislation reduced the government's control over nuclear energy technology and strengthened private initiatives for developing nuclear power. Within three years of enactment of the new act, the first U.S. power reactor demonstrated the technological feasibility of civilian nuclear energy, and privately owned plants soon followed. With extensive government support, industry made rapid advances in "scaling up" LWR technologies into commercial-size plants.[21] In December 1963, General Electric announced plans to build a turnkey nuclear power plant capable of producing economically competitive energy at Oyster Creek, New Jersey.[22]

The domestic and international programs launched in 1954 were interdependent. The ability to achieve the foreign policy goals of the peaceful atom was linked to the creation of technologically viable and, eventually, economically competitive civilian LWR. The United States could not undertake a policy of international nuclear cooperation in the peaceful uses of the atom without a competitive domestic technological base in nuclear energy technology and materials. Private sector interest in the new technology would not last without commercial applications on the horizon. The continuing attractiveness of American technology and material, from the first bilateral agreements for cooperation to the commercialization of LWRs and the domination of the civilian nuclear power plant market, leveraged U.S. nonproliferation policy and ensured support for the policy by a powerful domestic stakeholder.[23]

The pattern of U.S.-Swedish relations in civilian nuclear technology corresponds with American use of technology as part of a nonproliferation policy strategy. In addition to a research reactor and enriched fuel, in the mid-1950s the AEC provided a host of other forms of technical assistance.[24] In addition, as early as 1956, the United States and Sweden began discussions for more substantial cooperation governing future power reactor technology. Negotiating a power reactor agreement began in earnest in 1962 and was concluded in 1966.[25] Over time, these incentives helped dissuade Sweden from developing the technological capability to produce nuclear weapons.

Sweden's Domestic Situation: Incentives and Shifting Preferences

In the 1940s and 1950s, the pursuit of nuclear technology (military and civilian) attracted Sweden.[26] As one leading policymaker phrased it during the "heroic days" of Sweden's ambitions, nuclear energy held the promise of breaking Sweden's oil dependence and replacing it with a clean, efficient source that relied on Sweden's considerable technological competence. Nuclear energy also held the promise of fulfilling the Social Democrats' vision of effective government control over energy and industry.[27] Furthermore, Swedish society had no moral or environmental objections to nuclear power, at least not until the mid-1950s.[28] Sweden also saw the clear military possibilities of nuclear power from U.S. use of the bomb during World War II.[29] After the war, Sweden's leaders concluded that neutrality and national rearmament had worked[30] and that in the postwar world, Sweden would have to rely on its own resources and the concept of "total defense."[31] As part of that approach, many in Sweden assumed that nuclear weapons would soon be part of the Swedish arsenal, and, because the nuclear powers would not sell it nuclear weapons, that Sweden would need to manufacture nuclear material for a bomb itself.

During this period it did not appear that Sweden faced insuperable technical obstacles in acquiring the expertise and material for nuclear weapons development as a by-product of its civilian nuclear energy program. In 1945, Sweden's National Defense Research Institute (FOA) began nuclear weapons research and quickly concluded that plutonium should be the preferred material for atomic weapons.[32] In 1947, Sweden launched its civilian atomic energy program by creating a public-private company, Aktiebolaget (AB) Atomenergi, to promote nuclear energy, develop methods for uranium production, and begin work on a research reactor. The new company assumed control over nonmilitary nuclear research but cooperated closely with FOA.[33] In fact, declassified information revealed that in 1950 the Swedish cabinet approved a secret memorandum of agreement regulating the exchange of information and personnel between the military and civilian organizations "to avoid duplication and to coordinate efforts in a joint plan."[34] These decisions reflected the government's early conclusion that Sweden could not keep the pursuit of the atom's peaceful and military applications separate. Economic costs and finite technological resources required coordination of the civil and military programs.[35]

In pursuing its civilian energy goals, Sweden's initial preference was for a program based on potentially self-supporting natural uranium and HWRs that could also serve as the basis for its military needs.[36] Sweden's political leadership in the early 1950s recognized that an ability to produce atomic weapons would be a potential by-product of the civilian program through the development of nuclear expertise and the possibility of extracting and reprocessing spent civilian reactor fuel into weapons-grade plutonium outside of foreign control, inspection, or restriction.[37] Indeed, although the official motives were exclusively civilian (a rationale still defended by some today),[38] others have argued that the production of weapons-grade plutonium took priority over efforts to create electric power at that time.[39]

The creation of an independent nuclear program served Sweden's military aspirations. In 1948, Sweden's supreme commander instructed FOA to investigate the feasibility of developing nuclear weapons and nuclear propulsion in Sweden and the possible time frame for such a program. FOA concluded that developing sufficient plutonium for nuclear weapons cores would require a large HWR and would take between eight and thirteen years. Thus, it was important that the civilian reactor program make progress toward the goal of successful reactor design and maintain the military's secret link to the civilian reactor program over that period.[40] The 1950 agreement between FOA and AB Atomenergi to share resources and coordinate their efforts helped secure this link.[41]

By the early 1950s some branches of the Swedish armed services began openly advocating acquiring tactical nuclear weapons,[42] and by 1954, the Swedish military had come out squarely for the rapid development of tactical nuclear weapons, placing the issue at the forefront of Swedish political debate.[43] The military's proposal set off a storm of political debate in the Swedish Parliament and press. Until this time, a Swedish nuclear weapons program was not a political issue—officially no such program existed.

Because of lack of consensus within the ruling Social Democratic party on the issue, the government publicly demurred on the question of nuclear weapons acquisition. Behind the scenes, however, the joint civilian-military nuclear program took a large step forward. That step was Sweden's decision to develop large heavy water plutonium-producing reactors.[44] The decision, publicly made for civilian purposes, was supported by a detailed FOA study of the premises for developing nuclear weapons, which concluded that the best course of action remained a dual-purpose program where reactors would produce heat and electricity for civilian purposes and plutonium for military ones. Under this plan, Sweden would soon have a modest HWR producing plutonium at Agesta, then a larger reactor at Marviken.

In 1957, the issue of nuclear weapons returned to test the Social Democrats when FOA's director asked for a determination whether the military researchers could rely on planned civilian power reactors as a military resource to construct a nuclear weapon by 1963–64. To prevent the nuclear arms issue from dividing the party and dissolving the government (the Social Democrats governed with a single seat plurality in association with the Communist party), the party organized a special group of eighteen leaders to examine the issue in November 1958. The Committee for the Study of the Atomic Weapons Question, composed of weapons opponents and supporters from within the party and chaired by Prime Minister Tage Erlander, recommended postponing a definite decision on nuclear weapons acquisition until 1963–64, when Sweden would have the technical capability and nuclear material from its reactors for manufacturing nuclear weapons. The committee endorsed an expanded program of FOA "protective research," that is, "an investigation into all aspects of atomic weapons that might be of value for the development of protective devices and measures to be used by the military as well as the civilian population."[45] The decision was viewed by nuclear weapons proponents as a green light to continue working to reduce the time between a decision to build nuclear weapons and their actual production, whereas opponents to nuclear weapons acquisition considered it a way of gaining time to let resistance grow.[46] It also created a window of opportunity for American technological influence. While the decision unified the party, nuclear weapons–related research designed to produce a nuclear weapon on short notice continued outside the public eye (but not unknown to U.S. intelligence),[47] consistent with plans in place since the early 1950s.[48]

By the spring of 1961, FOA reported to the defense staff that most theoretic problems concerning the construction of a nuclear charge had been solved and that a simple prototype could be assembled if the necessary weapons-grade material could become available.[49] "The research program at FOA had obviously been following the original plans fairly well."[50] For Sweden to achieve its military aspirations, "all that was needed was for the civilian program to keep pace with the military one."[51]

The civilian side of Sweden's nuclear program was not keeping pace, however, straining the linkage between the civilian and military programs. The Agesta and Marviken HWRs under development by AB Atomenergi and the State Power Board were facing delays, cost overruns, and technological problems. The completion date for Agesta was delayed from 1961 to 1963 and then to 1964, and the cost of the project nearly doubled. The delays at Agesta meant it had fallen behind the schedule set by the defense staff for the production of militarily useful plutonium. Marviken experienced similar delays and cost overruns. "Altogether, this finally led to doubts about the whole HWR program in comparison with the emerging light-water reactor systems."[52] Marviken became unjustifiable except for its role in the fuel cycle for the production of militarily useful materials.[53]

As James Jasper writes, "Mild disenchantment with the Swedish heavy water line was reinforced by the rising tide of enthusiasm for LWRs emanating from the United States and advancing across Europe."[54] News of the American breakthrough to commercially competitive light water nuclear electricity at Oyster Creek spread quickly among the international nuclear energy community.[55] The technical problems at Marviken had weakened the Swedish government's role and strengthened the hand of private industry, such as ASEA, which preferred the LWR approach.

Sweden's nuclear power preferences and planning began shifting to LWRs. By the early 1960s, Sweden's power companies had concluded that delays in the domestic program would force them to purchase foreign reactor technology rather than wait for domestic models. The reliance of these imported reactors on safeguarded enriched fuel was of no concern to the utilities.[56]

The Swedish power utilities were eager to obtain experience in constructing and operating LWRs. The government insistence on the HWR approach adopted in the 1950s made little sense considering current technologies. The U.S. AEC had eliminated Sweden's early doubts regarding supply of enrichment services through the offer of a long-term fuel supply. By 1962, the AEC and Sweden were in serious negotiations over the transfer of reactor technology and fuel for large-scale power production,[57] which included a U.S. offer of long-term, low-cost guaranteed fuel supplies and LWR technology. Negotiations on this point culminated in a new cooperation agreement in 1966 under which the United States would supply enriched uranium, under safeguards, for the first of six Swedish nuclear power units up to the year 1996.[58]

The emerging Swedish reactor industry, in particular the Swedish firm ASEA, lobbied AB Atomenergi hard and successfully for scuttling the heavy line of reactors in favor of light water designs.[59] The American incentive strategy had mobilized an important recipient ally that stood to gain from the new technology and that would exercise its influence in reshaping the recipient state's preferences. In 1964, the State Power Board withdrew from the Marviken project. ASEA, meanwhile, had adapted its technology to LWR design and sold its first LWR to a Swedish electric utility consortium in 1965. The withdrawal of support by the state and private utilities sealed the fate of the Swedish HWRs. Even in FOA, the view by 1963–65 was that Sweden would not acquire nuclear weapons, although some nuclear-related research continued.[60]

Although Sweden had enough fuel from Agesta and sufficient reprocessing capabilities to manufacture a Nagasaki-class weapon by 1965, politically, it had tabled the issue, economically, the larger project had become immeasurably expensive, and militarily, opinion shifted in support of conventional forces rather than nuclear weapons to effectively keep the peace.[61] The Swedish nuclear weapons option died sometime during the mid-1960s. In February 1968, Parliament dryly stated: "It is not in our country's political interest to acquire nuclear weapons." In 1970, AB Atomenergi formally canceled the Marviken reactor because of design problems. Swedish authorities also closed Agesta. Out of economic, technological, and political necessity, Sweden turned to American-safeguarded enriched uranium fuel and power stations relying on LWR technology.[62]

The United States monitored Swedish developments closely, and its technology transfers were purposeful.[63] Consistent with its political and commercial interests, the United States sold LWRs and safeguarded materials to influence Sweden in stopping the proliferation danger posed by operating HWRs in countries with nuclear weapons potential.[64] The United States aimed its offers at making LWRs the sole economic choice for energy production by using technology transfer and concessionary long-term contracts on U.S.-controlled uranium as a barrier to nuclear weapons proliferation: "In effect the bargains offered by the U.S. AEC had quietly undone a Swedish defense plan."[65] As an AEC official at the center of the policy confided, "We made sure no one left the reservation."[66]

A nation's decision to adopt or forgo nuclear weapons is a function of both technological capability and political motivation. As Mitchell Reiss notes, "The capability without the motivation is innocuous. The motivation without the capability is futile."[67] Despite its technological competence, Sweden did not realize its weapons potential. Except for its initial research reactor and a small demonstration reactor at Agesta, Sweden's nuclear energy program became thoroughly dependent on American technology and material that prohibited Sweden from using them for making nuclear weapons or conducting nuclear weapons research.[68] In considering the impact of U.S. policies on Swedish decisions, Jerome Garris concludes: "Sweden's own civilian atomic energy setbacks and the policy of the United States in providing controlled nuclear materials ensured that Sweden's nuclear weapons capability was never very well developed."[69]

The lack of technologically and economically successful nuclear reactors meant that the plutonium needed for the nuclear weapons program was not available. The decoupling of the civilian and military nuclear programs made weapons procurement technologically more difficult and vastly more expensive. By the mid-1960s such a commitment was no longer a politically or militarily attractive option. Jan Prawitz, special assistant for disarmament at FOA at that time, summarized the nuclear situation facing Sweden in the early 1960s, "A number of economically motivated steps had made most of the civil atomic power program incompatible with military co-production and, practically speaking, over the years almost added up to a 'silent no' to the Swedish bomb."[70]

Politically, despite the perception that nuclear weapons could strengthen Sweden's security and neutrality, Sweden's domestic politics and the position and prominence of the Social Democratic party throughout the debate constrained weapons development. For internal reasons the party remained officially uncommitted to the nuclear option even if its leaders continued to keep the option available in secret. The party's decision not to decide on nuclear weapons during the 1950s was the only logical and politically prudent alternative. In effect, the decision constrained the probomb forces in and out of government and drove the research program underground.

Importantly, America's technologically and economically attractive alternative for civilian nuclear power helped insure that the military option did not resurface. Delaying the decision also permitted the enthusiasm for nuclear weapons within the party and the military to eventually wane,[71] and the Social Democratic resistance to nuclear weapons strengthened in the 1960s.[72]

Increasingly, forces in the international environment also inhibited the adoption of nuclear weapons including the likely negative impact of an affirmative nuclear weapons decision on Sweden's relations with the Soviet Union and its Scandinavian neighbors.[73] Strategically, the warfare advantages of tactical nuclear forces steadily declined against the growing size and sophistication of superpower nuclear and conventional arsenals[74] as the international norm of nuclear nonproliferation grew.

In sum, American peaceful nuclear technology transfer that inhibited weapons development came during a critical period when the political and security environment made the nuclear option most attractive when technological capability factors might have swayed decisions.[75] American policies, including civilian nuclear technology incentives, encouraged Sweden to abandon its HWR approach, shift its preference to LWRs, and forgo the possibility of an independent military nuclear capability in the 1960s.

CHAPTER 4

Trade and Technology Transfer to the People's Republic of China, 1978–86

From Embargo to Incentives: Changing the Strategic Environment

The United States's incentive program toward China followed a long period of embargo that began in 1949. As the Chinese communists advanced south through the mainland and their victory over the Nationalist government became imminent, the United States stopped shipments of goods it feared would help increase the strength of communist armed forces.[1] Later that year, as the communists solidified control over the mainland, the United States imposed stringent controls over petroleum, metal, chemical, and industrial equipment exports. These restrictions matched those the United States had in place against the Soviet bloc.[2] Immediately preceding China's involvement in the Korean conflict, the United States substantially expanded the list of embargoed items, seized Chinese assets in the United States, denied most favored nation (MFN) treatment to Chinese imports, and withdrew Export-Import Bank financing.[3] The centerpiece of the American embargo was the cutoff of American exports to the PRC under authority vested in the president by the Export Control Act of 1949 as reinforced by the Mutual Defense Assistance Act (or Battle Act), which permitted a cutoff in U.S. aid to countries violating U.S. embargo policies. To further its export embargo policy, the United States eventually enlisted the support of its European allies and Japan through the Coordinating Committee for Multilateral Export Controls (COCOM).[4]

After Korea, American policymakers asserted that the embargo should isolate China diplomatically and damage it economically.[5] The embargo was both a means of containing communist expansion and a way to weaken and delegitimize communist rule, thereby creating conditions for its eventual collapse or overthrow. From the outset, the U.S. government professed the belief that communist rule in China ran contrary to

China's true national interests and identity and therefore would not endure. The government defended the embargo against China as an effective counterrevolutionary strategy. Even after China began to assert independence from the Soviet line, American policymakers spoke of the expected demise of Chinese communism.

By 1960 economic advancement and political stability in China had undercut much of this rationale. U.S. policymakers increasingly justified U.S. sanctions as symbolically important, even if not instrumental to the removal of communism in China. They stressed that relaxing economic sanctions against China would damage the credibility of U.S. policy, which had branded China and Maoist revolutionary doctrines as a threat to U.S. interests, and would unleash allied pressure to seek further accommodation with Beijing.[6]

Allied and American business frustration with U.S. policies mounted in the 1960s.[7] Continuation of a largely symbolic embargo was economically costly to U.S. exporters and contributed to frictions between the United States and its allies whenever the United States attempted to press them to bring their policies into line with the United States's.[8] The U.S. worsening balance-of-payments position, unemployment concerns, and growing competition from Japan and Europe underscored the problem.

The movement away from sanctions did not begin until the Nixon administration, however. On taking office, President Nixon directed Henry Kissinger and the National Security Council (NSC) to explore avenues for signaling a relaxation in U.S. policies toward China. The United States permitted limited tourist visits and, in April 1970, began to license the export of selective American-made, nonstrategic goods to China. By March 1971, the State Department dropped all restrictions on travel to China, and three weeks later China invited an American table tennis team competing in Japan to visit for a series of exhibition matches.[9]

Responding immediately to China's hospitality, Nixon announced six additional relaxations in U.S. sanctions. The most significant was a directive to the NSC to draw up a list of nonstrategic goods that could be freely exported to China. Following the preparation of the list, the government authorized selective imports from China.[10] One month later came the surprising news that Premier Zhou Enlai had invited President Nixon to visit China and that Nixon would go there by May 1972 to seek normalization of relations.

In explaining the new direction in U.S. policy, administration officials pointed to a recalculation of the nature of the strategic threat posed by China: "[The threat] is less direct than many supposed it earlier to be and the capacity to deal with the threat, especially among China's non-Communist neighbors, is generally greater than in the 1950s."[11] Specifically,

American policymakers increasingly viewed the Sino-Soviet schism and the emerging power of Japan as creating counterweights to Chinese influence that, except for the ongoing war in Vietnam, did not pose a direct threat to Southeast Asia.

China was reassessing the international environment as well. The Soviet invasion of Czechoslovakia in 1968 and Sino-Soviet border clashes in 1969 led China's leaders to emphasize the security threat from the Soviet Union rather than the West. Moreover, some Chinese leaders were beginning to see the United States as useful for its emerging economic strategy.

After Nixon's visit, the two countries announced the first major thaw in U.S. embargo policy in the Shanghai Communiqué of 1972 wherein "[b]oth sides viewed bilateral trade as another area from which mutual benefits [could] be derived, and agree[d] that economic relations based on equality and mutual benefit [were] in the interest of the people of the two countries."[12] The communiqué officially marked the resumption of commercial relations between the United States and China. The United States relaxed trade restrictions with China to the same level as with the USSR, a policy of "evenhandedness" in economic relations. Despite some early enthusiasm, the growth in U.S.-PRC trade was slow and uneven.[13]

China's policies toward the United States mirrored the American embargo and its relaxation. China, too, initially subordinated economic relations with the West to ideological and political imperatives. Before the Western embargo, Mao Zedong, in a speech delivered to the Chinese Communist Party (CCP) Central Committee in June 1949, spurned U.S. and British aid and announced his "lean-to-one-side" policy, saying, "We belong to the side of the anti-imperialist front headed by the Soviet Union and so we turn only to this side for genuine and friendly help."[14] Mao's decision to lean toward the Soviet Union was motivated by both domestic and foreign policy considerations. Carol Lee Hamrin explains:

> Close cooperation with the Soviet Union . . . provided a protective umbrella to deter U.S. or Japanese hostilities while facilitating improvements of China's military and security forces; it provided a ready-made socialist development model, accompanied by advisors, blueprints, training, some assistance, and large loans; and it added international status to the CCP's leadership credentials and diplomatic backing for efforts to replace the Nationalists in the U.N. and other international organizations.[15]

The commitment of Chinese troops to the Korean conflict in October 1950 severed most of China's economic relations with the West and the United States.

China's collectivized economic development strategy during this postrevolutionary period followed that of the Soviet Union—China's chief benefactor.[16] During the 1950s, the Soviet Union, and its allies, became China's chief trading partner. Trade with the Soviet bloc accounted for 65.3 percent of China's total trade, as China's trade with Eastern Europe grew steadily throughout the decade. Trade with the West constituted a very small share of China's economic exchange, and U.S.-China trade virtually ceased by 1954.[17]

The economic and political chaos of Mao's Great Leap Forward (1958–60), which sought to accelerate economic growth and egalitarianism in China (a principle Mao believed Stalin and Khrushchev had abandoned), would exacerbate ideological and geopolitical disputes with the Soviets and, eventually, force a divorce between the two nations. In August 1960 the Soviet Union severed its economic and technical support for China's economic development projects. As a result, China turned inward to adjust its development policies during the 1960s and became more self-reliant in its dealings with the outside world. Although China did not withdraw into autarky—its overall trade was increasing, for example—China's foreign economic relations remained at arm's length to lessen China's contact with foreign societies.[18]

By 1971 a new policy line began to emerge in China, led by Zhou Enlai and Deng Xiaoping, that favored moving away from self-reliance toward greater importation of foreign goods and technology to speed China's development and modernization. China's technological isolation left it ten to forty years behind the West as the Soviet and Eastern European technology base that had been transferred to China in the mid-1950s decayed. The Chinese estimated that 60 percent of their industrial technology was completely obsolete or worn out by the late 1970s.[19]

To remedy this problem, China began trading more with the West and increased its involvement in world affairs. Zhou endorsed bilateral economic relations with the United States and Japan, despite both countries' recognition of Taiwan. During 1972–78, China's trade with the West tripled, and Western nations accounted for 28.5 percent of China's trade.[20] Opposition from radical Maoists within the government ensured that consolidation and implementation of this new direction would not come until 1979, after Deng had won the endorsement of the CCP Central Committee and solidified his political control.

Moving Toward Cooperation: China

Although progress was not dramatic, the outlines of greater Sino-American cooperation took shape in the 1970s. Early in the decade, the United

States had begun a strategic reassessment of its relationship with China and had removed barriers to more normal commercial relations. As yet, the United States did not feel compelled to offer China the economic incentives that were uniquely important to the PRC—access to U.S. and Western high technology, the U.S. market, and Western capital. China, in turn, had not yet firmly committed itself to a plan of economic development and engagement with the West that would make such incentives a compelling factor in its relations with the United States.[21]

By the late 1970s, however, conditions for the effective use of American economic incentives were in place. In 1978 Deng and the reformers relaunched the Four Modernizations Policy first proposed by Zhou but shelved in the mid-1970s. The modernizations plan sought to revitalize the Chinese economy in agriculture, industry, national defense, and science and technology by the year 2000. Crucial to the program's success was an "opening to the West" to obtain the goods and services necessary for the modernization process. In addition, the Chinese were willing to finance their imports with loans from Western financial institutions for the first time.[22] Clearly, China placed a higher utility on Western technology and trade than it had in the past.

At the Third Plenary Session of the Eleventh Central Committee of the CCP in December 1978, the party officially endorsed the Four Modernizations. The party would devote itself fully to the goal of China's modernization rather than class struggle. As part of this "historic turning point" (as the PRC phrased its decision), the party announced that China would be "actively expanding economic cooperation on terms of mutual benefit with other countries" and would be "striving to adopt the world's advanced technologies and equipment."[23] Full implementation of the program began when Deng purged the remaining Maoists and gained full control over the CCP Central Committee in 1979.

The emergence of the reformers as the dominant political actors led to economic and structural changes in China. Chinese policy shifted from building egalitarian socialism to an emphasis on economic construction. Many of the reforms increased China's interactions with the international economy. China began to implement policies premised on the belief that foreign technology and capital were necessary to modernize China and to maintain a high level of economic growth.[24]

China quickly gave the Open Door concrete meaning. By July 1979, China had promulgated a new "Law of the People's Republic of China on Joint Ventures," a significant step in confirming its Open Door policy. Foreign trade with technologically advanced countries skyrocketed in the 1978–85 period. China began to accept foreign aid, loans, and credit. Chinese scholars were increasingly sent abroad for technical training and research. In 1982, a new constitution legalized and protected foreign investment. China also created a new joint venture law and special economic zones (SEZs) to encourage foreign investment and technology transfer.[25]

Moving Toward Cooperation: The United States

The United States, meanwhile, was reassessing China's strategic importance and economic needs and would fashion an economic incentive program to encourage closer strategic cooperation between the two countries. For the incoming Carter administration, fuller normalization of relations with China was a goal that would gather momentum in the late 1970s. In December 1976, incoming Secretary of State Cyrus Vance established a group of China specialists within the executive branch to examine the normalization issue (the "China Group"). Vance believed that diplomatic ties should "be accompanied by a gradual but careful expansion of the economic relationship" so as not to upset the Soviet Union.[26] Consistent with this concern (and that of Taiwan's security), the China Group recommended a gradual move toward normalization.[27]

Carter's national security adviser, Zbigniew Brzezinski, who would come to dominate China policy within the administration, favored a more aggressive policy of expanding economic ties "so that both countries would have a stake in tangible benefits" and the development of strategic cooperation with China. Brzezinski believed that economic exchange with China would lay the groundwork for improved Sino-American security relations and a further deterioration in the Sino-Soviet link.[28]

Brzezinski's proposal for expanded bilateral scientific contacts and a more favorable attitude toward the transfer of militarily sensitive technology received Carter's endorsement.[29] A special NSC interagency committee was created "for a more positive handling of Chinese [technology] requests," for example.[30] As NSC China expert Michael Oksenberg noted, the February decision dovetailed with events in Beijing where the National People's Congress "placed economic development at the top of China's agenda. This significantly enhanced the attractiveness of a closer relationship with the United States for the technology and capital it could offer."[31]

By April 1978 Brzezinski had arranged his own trip to China. Carter's instructions to Brzezinski authorized him to offer "to widen the opportunities for commercial flow of technology to China . . . and to invite China's trade and military delegations to visit the United States."[32] Trade and technology incentives were to be important indicia of the seriousness of U.S. intentions.

In his May discussion with the Chinese leaders in Beijing, Brzezinski proposed that the two nations exchange trade delegations and hinted at the possible relaxation of high technology restrictions. Brzezinski reported China's keen interest in his promise of expanded commercial exchange. He noted that Vice Premier Deng repeatedly "stressed China's interest in obtaining greater access to American technology," but Deng remained concerned that the United States would not deliver on its promises "for fear of offending the Soviets." Brzezinski strongly denied any such inhibition.[33] As a product of the discussion, both sides agreed not to contradict one another in statements over the future of Taiwan. A series of negotiations followed.

In November, Vice Premier Deng told Western reporters of his desire to visit the United States. In a statement meant to reassure U.S. businesses with operations in Taiwan, he publicly announced in December that China would not object to continued U.S.-Taiwanese economic ties. By mid-December, a U.S.-PRC normalization agreement was ready, and Carter announced the decision, with little forewarning to Congress. Vice Premier Deng arrived in Washington the following month.[34]

The next step in U.S. incentive strategy was the granting of MFN treatment to China. The granting of MFN, in essence treating Chinese imports like those of GATT members for tariff purposes, was an important part of the trade package negotiated with China and signed by the two countries in July 1979. Carter waived the prohibitions on China's receipt of MFN[35] and submitted the Sino-American trade treaty to Congress in October 1979. Carter intended economic measures to strengthen broader political and strategic cooperation over time. Economic benefits offered to China would, in Carter's words, "give further impetus to the progress we have made in our overall relationship since normalization."[36] Congress endorsed the president's action, approving the treaty in January 1980. The MFN agreement led to an acceleration in U.S.-China trade—from $2.45 billion in 1979 to $6.85 billion in 1981—and broke the policy of even-handedness in U.S. relations with the two communist powers.[37]

The United States also altered the policy of evenhandedness in technology transfer by promoting the export to China of dual-use technology not available for export to the Soviet Union.[38] Although publicly denying American intentions to develop a military relationship with China, Vice President Walter Mondale, in his August 1979 visit to Beijing, privately informed the Chinese that the Carter Administration had begun serious consideration of a policy that would differentiate the PRC from the USSR on controls governing exports of high technology transfer.[39] The two sides also agreed at that time that Secretary of Defense Harold Brown would visit Beijing in January 1980.

On the eve of Brown's trip (December 27, 1979), the Soviet Union invaded Afghanistan. Carter allegedly viewed the invasion as a fundamental violation of understandings that had implicitly governed U.S.-USSR relations since World War II, and he used Brown's trip to announce increased U.S. flexibility regarding sales of high technology to the PRC.[40] During his trip, the first by a U.S. secretary of defense since 1949, Brown officially announced a new tilt in U.S. policy, one in which the United States would consider, on a case-by-case basis, sales to China of advanced dual-use technology not available for export to the USSR. Shortly thereafter, the U.S. Defense Department indicated it would sell certain non-lethal military support equipment, such as early warning radars, to China.[41] The policy signaled a new stage in Sino-American strategic relations. Richard Holbrooke, Assistant Secretary of State for Asia and Pacific Affairs, offered this contemporary assessment of U.S. policy: "In the first phase, we recognized each other. . . . In the second phase, we tried to put our non-diplomatic, bilateral relations on a normal basis. . . . The third phase began with Secretary Brown's trip, and [the movement of] the bilateral relations into discussion of broad strategic issues of mutual interest."[42]

In April 1980, the Carter administration created new, less restrictive guidelines for technology exports to the PRC.[43] The guidelines, issued shortly before the 1980 U.S. presidential election, were not implemented immediately by the bureaucracy, however, as they waited for a policy decision from the incoming Reagan administration. In March 1981, Secretary of State Alexander Haig reassured a wary Chinese government of the new U.S. president's commitment to relaxing high technology controls.[44] In June 1981, President Ronald Reagan followed the Carter administration's decision to relax U.S. export controls by issuing a directive allowing for approval of technology and equipment exports to China at levels generally twice those approved for the USSR—the so-called two-times policy.[45]

Problems of implementation immediately followed the two-times decision, however, and continued after the policy's promulgation. Responding to the complaints of American exporters and the Chinese government, in May 1983 President Reagan announced a new policy of treating China like other Western nations for most high technology exports.[46] The China case perhaps best illustrates the mobilization of sender state interest groups (American exporters) to bolster the endurance of an incentive program. It also demonstrates the importance of institutional implementation to give incentives maximum effect.

The implementation of the 1983 reforms led to a rapid growth in technology transfer.[47] The number of export license applications and the value of technology approved for export to China expanded rapidly: license applications more than doubled between 1983 and 1985 from 4,300 to

10,200, and the value of licensed exports grew tenfold from $374 million in 1980 to $3,366 million in 1986.[48]

Incentives and Bilateral Cooperation

Although directed toward the achievement of several objectives, the over-arching purpose of U.S. policy was to protect and enhance Sino-American political and strategic cooperation by giving the Chinese an economic and technological stake in preserving good relations with the United States and the West. A 1979 Pentagon study, "Consolidated Guidance Number 8: Asia During a Worldwide Conventional War," spelled out U.S. strategy. The report recommended that the United States strengthen China's defense capability and support its modernization effort through expanded economic and technology exchange. The report specified policies that would further this strategy, including the provision of high technology, defense equipment, intelligence, licensing of U.S. weapons, and joint military exercise—all of which would become part of the bilateral relationship over the next several years.[49]

Scholars and analysts who have considered U.S. policy during this period also identify America's strategic intentions. Tan Qingshan summarized U.S. policy goals:

> The first objective was to develop strategic cooperation. A better relationship with China would enable the United States to win a de facto ally against Soviet global expansion, especially in the face of the Afghanistan invasion. The second was to stabilize Asian affairs. Better Sino-U.S. relations could serve as a balance of forces in Asia favorable to the United States and its allies and friends in the region and help stabilize the situation on the Korean peninsula. The last was to gain political and economic benefits. A good bilateral relationship would benefit the United States from economic, cultural, and other exchanges.[50]

In testimony to the U.S. Congress in 1982, Robert Sutter described the anticipated return on assisting in China's economic modernization as "strengthening the already close security collaboration between the United States and China." Sutter added, "Peking would remain preoccupied with domestic development, solicitous of its non-communist neighbors, and unlikely to pursue ideological causes of the past that might compromise practical contemporary interests in modernization and development. A continuation of China's moderate stance on Taiwan would be expected under these circumstances."[51]

Although the level of cooperation between China and the United States varied over time and across issue areas, in several important arenas China adjusted its foreign policy in a cooperative fashion influenced in part by its interest in securing and expanding its economic and technological link to the United States and the West.

In many respects, U.S. and Chinese goals were harmonious. The goals were far from identical, however. A basic complementary (rather than identity) between U.S. and PRC interests is the underlying basis for cooperation. As noted, security motivated the United States. The United States also had a complementary economic logic to its security policy "which sought not simply an anti-Soviet China but also a China that would be, for the foreseeable future, enmeshed with and dependent upon the U.S.-managed world economy."[52] From the Chinese perspective, economic concerns took highest priority by the late 1970s and 1980s. China's leaders emphasized "economic diplomacy," that is, China should use its foreign policy to serve the nation's paramount interest—economic development. This economic emphasis encouraged Beijing to seek a stable and peaceful international environment so China would not divert its energies from the goal of economic modernization. As Deng Xiaoping succinctly said, "China needs at least 20 years of peace to concentrate on our domestic development."[53] This approach to foreign relations encouraged greater pragmatism and a willingness to find common ground with the United States and other states on an issue-by-issue basis.[54] Thus, the shared goals in constraining Soviet influence and in expanded commercial ties should not obfuscate their different preferences and their cooperative adjustments made in view of the other's primary interest. Roger Sullivan, former assistant secretary of state in charge of China policy, describes the trade-off as follows:

> This is not to minimize the importance of geopolitical factors in the normalization process. China, of course, shared in the U.S. interest in resisting Soviet power. The United States shared China's interest in the economic benefits of normal relations. *But the economic benefits were primary in China's eyes. For the Americans the strategic and geopolitical gains were predominant.* It is in this complementarity of interests that the significance and implications of the growing United States–China economic relationship can be found.[55]

By the late 1970s, China's foreign policy sought to strengthen its strategic and economic ties with the United States against the Soviet Union in part to secure Western and U.S. capital and technology and markets. The PRC first demonstrated the depth of its interest in improved economic relations with the United States in its willingness to normalize relations with the United States despite U.S. assertions that it would continue to sell weapons to Taiwan.[56] Other less dramatic evidence of Chinese accommodation with the United States and the West included the elimination of its rhetorical support for a "new international economic order" and the removal of the United States from its list of hegemonic powers (leaving the Soviet Union and its allies).

By 1980–81, cooperation between the two countries had expanded in the strategic and economic spheres. Notably, the United States and China began to coordinate policy on regional issues. The PRC sought to align itself with the United States over continuation of the Japanese-American security relationship, maintenance of peace on the Korean peninsula, and opposition to Vietnam's invasion of Cambodia. The two countries also began limited cooperation in security affairs—the United States relaxing restrictions on military equipment sales and China agreeing to establish a joint surveillance facility to monitor Soviet missile tests.[57]

The evolution of U.S.-PRC relations was not one of unremitting progress. This case illustrates several important limits to cooperation. Several irritants contributed to a cooling in Sino-American relations during 1981–83.[58] Further, a divergent reappraisal by the United States and China over the nature of the Soviet threat and the importance of Sino-American strategic cooperation slowed cooperation. The Reagan administration came into office perceiving an immediate need to directly challenge Soviet military capabilities. The result was to diminish in the eyes of the American executive the importance of the PRC in redressing Soviet military advantages. By 1981–82, China, in contrast, appears to have concluded that the Soviet threat had lessened because of Soviet difficulties in Afghanistan and Eastern Europe and economic problems at home. Yet, given the high level of U.S.-Soviet tension, China's strategic alignment toward the United States tempted a Soviet preemptive action against China or, at a minimum, could have required greater defense preparedness by Beijing.[59] Thus, the PRC saw a diminished need for strategic cooperation with the West. Yet, "good relations with the United States would remain very important, especially if China were to benefit more fully in the areas of economic collaboration and technology transfer."[60] On balance, China's common economic and security interests with the United States would continue to outweigh those between China and the Soviet Union.[61]

A series of measures, including the promise and delivery of U.S. high technology, a compromise on arms sales to Taiwan, and the settlement of a textile dispute contributed to a second wave of bilateral cooperation in the years 1983–84. Recognizing the importance of access to U.S. and Western technology, capital, and expertise, the Chinese responded directly to the May 1983 announcement to ease technology transfer restrictions by agreeing to schedule a long-delayed visit by U.S. Defense Secretary Caspar Weinberger in September 1983. China's defense minister made a corresponding visit the next spring, followed by the visit of several teams of Chinese military experts to the United States to explore the possibility of military trade and assistance.[62] This process of reconciliation culminated in an exchange of visits between Premier Zhao and President Reagan in early 1984.

Although portrayed by Beijing as independent steps, it was clear that China was reviving defense cooperation and high-level political contacts and moderating demands and threats of retaliation over Taiwan for the sake of improved Sino-American economic relations. The cooperative adjustments by the PRC during this period included changing its policy on purchasing arms from the United States, soft-pedaling past demands and threats, joining the Asian Development Bank despite Taiwan's membership, and others.[63]

The slow but steady expansion of U.S.-PRC military links in the 1980s, despite China's view that the Soviet threat to the mainland was continuing to recede, is also significant. Coinciding with Reagan's liberalization of dual-use technology restrictions, in 1981 Secretary of State Alexander Haig announced that the United States would sell lethal military equipment to China.[64] By 1984, after a host of functional and high-level exchanges, the United States made China eligible for U.S. Foreign Military Sales, which granted the PRC access to U.S. military hardware and technology through government to government channels.[65] In early 1985, U.S. Joint Chiefs of Staff Chairman General John Vessey arrived in China to discuss military cooperation between the two nations. A preliminary understanding was reached on the question of selling American antisubmarine warfare equipment to China and on planned U.S. Navy port calls.[66] In 1986, the Chief of Staff of the People's Liberation Army (PLA) visited the United States—the first-ever such visit by the head of the Chinese military establishment. Secretary of Defense Weinberger returned the visit four months later as part of a high-level dialogue on security issues. More important, China and the United States set up active naval coordination links that year when PLA warships and units of the U.S. Pacific Fleet conducted joint communications and signaling exercises in the South China Sea. In November 1986, U.S. ships under the command of the U.S. Pacific Fleet commander, Admiral James Lyons, paid a courtesy visit at the port of Tsing Tao—the first by a U.S. warship since 1949. Despite Chinese efforts to keep the visit low-key, the message was not lost on the Soviet Union, which responded by simulating bombing attacks on the Alaskan and Chinese coasts.[67]

Considering these developments, some China scholars have asked: "Why did Peking move ahead with security cooperation with the United States just as it was becoming confident that the Soviets would not attack mainland China [and] a U.S. security link . . . was certain to antagonize Moscow?"[68] Analysts have concluded that China acceded to U.S. demands for active military links to guarantee access to U.S. technology and economic benefits essential to China's modernization.[69] Others have maintained that the United States made China's military cooperation a test of China's sincerity in opposing Soviet hegemony.[70] According to this analysis, China's refusal to cooperate could have adversely affected China's access to U.S. technology.[71]

Differences between the United States and China remained in the mid-1980s, but both sides recognized and worked with reasonable success in managing those differences to avoid serious interference in what they came to see as their mutually beneficial relationship: "the PRC gets a peaceful environment in which to develop . . . technology, access to the American market, and capital from international institutions and American investors. The United States gets strategic benefits."[72] As Harry Harding observed, China's stress on economic modernization and its growing economic interaction with the United States during this period "will give Peking a lasting incentive to manage and moderate any geopolitical tensions in its relationship with Washington. . . ."[73] This statement is not meant to imply that a strongly nationalistic power like China disregarded enduring problem areas in its relationship to Washington, only that it had a greater incentive to manage those conflicts with flexibility and patience.[74]

In short, the PRC took pains to ensure that its foreign policy did not jeopardize the flow of U.S. and Western technology, capital, and access to markets, and the United States delivered a measure of advanced technology and facilitated China's access to its market and to public and private capital to improve political and strategic cooperation with the PRC. Bilateral frictions and adjustments continued to be a part of Sino-American relations during this period. Overall, however, American economic incentives—markets, capital, and technology—broadened the cooperative interactions between the two countries, contributed to the achievement of their respective objectives, and produced a measure of cooperative "spillover" in their concurrent relations.

Although construction of an economic and technological foundation was critical in stabilizing the U.S.-PRC relationship in the 1980s, the tragic events in Tiananmen Square in June 1989 are a sobering reminder of the limits of foreign influence. The United States and the West lacked the means to stop a major alteration in Chinese domestic politics when China's leaders judged that suppression of their own people and alleged foreign ideas was essential to the survival of the regime. Thus, the PRC chose to incur significant diplomatic and economic costs to pursue a crackdown on internal democratic forces. In so doing, China's leaders severely disrupted a decade of carefully cultivated cooperation and integration with the West to exercise brutal repression of popular unrest at home.[75]

In matters of foreign policy also, improved technological and economic relations did not foreclose China's rhetoric stressing its independence from the United States or condemning American policies outside of the PRC's immediate sphere of interest.[76] The crisis surrounding the export of Chinese Silkworm missiles to Iran and the sale of intermediate-range ballistic missiles to Saudi Arabia illustrate that the U.S.-Chinese cooperation on specific global or regional problems by the late 1980s could not be assumed by the United States. Still, "due to America's energetic representations, China ceased sending silkworm missiles to Iran and instilled confidence that it would not ship intermediate ballistic missiles to others after its one-time deal with Saudi Arabia."[77] The economic importance of the United States to China ensured that U.S. concerns would be heard.

CHAPTER 5

Economic Incentives and Czechoslovakian Cooperation in the Nonproliferation of Dangerous Technology

U.S. Policy: From Containment to Nonproliferation

In the post–World War II era, regulating trade and technology and financial flows to the East was a straightforward proposition. The United States and its Western allies would prohibit most transactions to the Eastern bloc as the economic arm of the strategy of containment. The goal was to limit the economic and military potential of adversary nations. Czechoslovakia, a staunch supporter of the Soviet Union and its Warsaw Pact ally, was among the targets of the American-led embargo.

The United States prohibited loans and export credits to Czechoslovakia under the Johnson Debt Default Act of 1934.[1] In the area of trade, the United States had no trade agreement, high tariffs, and very little trade with Czechoslovakia in the post–World War II era.[2] In the late 1940s, Congress also passed export control legislation denying Czechoslovakia and other communist countries access to U.S. technology. With the help of other Western countries in the Coordinating Committee for Multilateral Export Controls (COCOM), the technology embargo became a multilateral prohibition on virtually all trade.[3] These prohibitions remained remarkably constant features of U.S. foreign economic policy from the 1950s through the 1980s.[4]

The end of the Cold War and the unrelenting East-West competition and hostility of the prior forty years forced a realignment of policy to meet new challenges. The basic Western security concern of a sudden Warsaw Pact attack on Western Europe or the more diffuse concern of a communist policy of radical activism in the Third World dissolved and was replaced by concerns over centrifugal tendencies and economic decay in these nations, or the possible export of dangerous technologies from former Eastern bloc states to unstable regimes.

The countries of Eastern and Central Europe and the former Soviet Union threatened international stability in a second way. Sudden oversupply and overcapacity in military and militarily related technology in the former Warsaw Pact was an unfortunate consequence of the Cold War's end. Czechoslovakia, a small country no longer part of a larger alliance, could not sustain its arms industries through purchases for its own forces or those within its alliance. Until the eventual conversion of these defense industries to civilian projects, arms producers in Czechoslovakia and elsewhere faced considerable economic pressure to export weapons and weapons-related technology to any potential buyer to earn foreign exchange and, ironically, to finance military conversion and economic modernization. Ensuring that Western technology was not retransferred to unstable areas and engendering responsible policies over arms manufacturing and exporting soon became an important aspect of U.S. nonproliferation policy toward Czechoslovakia.

Further, revolutions in Central and Eastern Europe and the newly independent states of the former Soviet Union required Western economic and technological assistance to replace command economies with market systems. Certain technologies, for example telecommunications and computers, were particularly important for promoting democratic pluralism and contributing to the establishment of modern production and financial systems. Access to Western markets and capital was equally essential to generate foreign exchange for imports and modernization. In short, the threat from the East was no longer conventional attack, but the regional instability that would ensue from the failure of nascent economic and political reforms.

The necessity of reintegrating Eastern European countries into the world economy, aiding the conversion of their military industries to civilian production, and gaining their cooperation in technology transfer became apparent when the West shifted its security focus from the diminishing possibility of East-West conflict to the growing reality of proliferation of weapons and dangerous technologies. As the former Cold War security concern evaporated, another replaced it: the spread of nuclear, chemical, biological, and conventional weapons and missile technology to dangerous regimes or unstable regions. By 1990, as many as twenty nations had or were acquiring chemical weapons capabilities, and missile delivery systems capable of carrying nuclear or chemical weapons were under development in as many as a dozen countries. Demand for weapons, coupled with overcapacity in the supply of military goods and technology following the end of the Cold War, created a growing market for dangerous technologies.

In addressing the problem of proliferation, the United States began working with its COCOM allies and other states like Czechoslovakia to encourage them to develop indigenous technology control systems and to join other multilateral export control arrangements. In addition to COCOM, the late 1980s saw the emergence of three independent multilateral regimes—the Nuclear Suppliers Group (NSG), the Missile Technology Control Regime (MTCR), and the Australia Group (AG)—that address the question of regulating dual-use technology for nuclear, missile, and chemical weapons, respectively. Strengthening nascent multilateral technology control regimes to combat the proliferation of dangerous technologies and expanding their membership to include countries like Czechoslovakia became an important goal of U.S. trade and technology transfer policy.[5]

A New American Strategy: Economic Incentives for Former Adversaries

In response to revolutions in Eastern Europe and pressure from allies for reform, by 1990 the United States began to establish a new policy toward the East. From 1990 through 1992, the United States made a strategic reassessment of the situation in Eastern Europe and offered the reform-minded countries of that region (Czechoslovakia, Hungary, and Poland) a new economic bargain—trade and technology incentives for responsible nonproliferation policies.

American economic incentives offered to Czechoslovakia during 1990–92 were extensive and represented a radical break with past policy. Within a few months of the 1989 Czech revolution, U.S. Secretary of State James Baker visited Czechoslovakia and described the U.S. intention to meet the economic needs of that country:

> We must integrate the new market democracies into the international economic system. You need access to the International Monetary Fund (IMF) and the World Bank resources. You need barriers to trade removed bilaterally and through the General Agreement on Tariffs and Trade (GATT) so potential investors will know they can export to other markets. You need access to high technology. To meet this need, the United States is considering with its allies adjustments in the Coordinating Committee for Multilateral Export Controls (COCOM) system that could enable you to have access to technology provided you will protect it and forgo industrial espionage.[6]

In fashioning policies to respond to these needs, Secretary Baker promised a litany of new economic incentives for Czechoslovakia, including temporary MFN status, Overseas Private Investment Corporation financing, Export-Import Bank and Commodity Credit Corporation financing, encouragement and support for private investment, and support for Czechoslovakia's membership in international financial organizations.[7]

That spring, the United States and Czechoslovakia entered into a landmark bilateral trade agreement—the first such agreement between the United States and an Eastern European country since the fall of communism. The agreement (which still required congressional approval), in conjunction with President Bush's decision in February 1990 to waive the Jackson-Vanik amendment for Czechoslovakia,[8] permitted goods produced in Czechoslovakia to enter the United States at MFN tariff rates—those established for America's preferred trading partners. Among other things, the granting of MFN made barter deals more attractive to U.S. exporters and investors because the bartered goods would have easier access to U.S. consumers.

When President Bush visited Czechoslovakia in late 1990, he concluded additional agreements "giving Czechoslovakia the fullest access to American markets, American investment, and American technology."[9] He promised prompt economic assistance to the nascent Czech private sector from a $370 million fund committed to Central and Eastern Europe and encouragement of American private-sector involvement in rebuilding Czech infrastructure. He also noted that the United States expected the IMF to lend—at U.S. urging—up to $5 billion in 1991 to Central and Eastern Europe and the World Bank to commit an additional $9 billion over the following three years.[10]

The American executive, Congress, and Western institutions[11] followed through on many of the promised initiatives. By December of the following year, Congress had passed and the president had signed legislation providing for permanent MFN status for Czechoslovakia, normalizing trade relations with that country. The legislation stated that the Jackson-Vanik provision would no longer apply to Czechoslovakia. The new legislation stipulated, however, that the president must issue a proclamation before the MFN status became permanent.[12] In signing the legislation, President Bush noted that the agreement would also normalize trade relations between the United States and Czechoslovakia under GATT and that it represented "a further important step on the way to full integration into the world market."[13]

In 1990 and 1991, two-way trade between the United States and Czechoslovakia increased more than 50 percent, from $178 million to $268 million.[14] During the first nine months of 1992, Czech imports from the United States rose an additional 25.5 percent, to $199 million, while exports to the United States jumped 74.9 percent, to $139 million.[15]

Remarking on the importance of the bilateral trade relationship for his country, Josef Baksay, the Czech foreign trade minister, said he would like to see the United States regain its previous position as a major trading partner, noting that before World War II the United States was Czechoslovakia's second-largest trading partner.[16]

As part of President Bush's Trade Enhancement Initiative for Central and Eastern Europe announced in July 1991, the United States went beyond granting MFN status and removed tariffs on certain Czech exports under the generalized system of preferences (GSP) program, which grants duty-free access to the United States for designated products from developing countries. As a result of a special review, the U.S. Trade Representative, which administers the GSP program, announced that eighty-three items from four Eastern European countries (Czechoslovakia, Bulgaria, Hungary, and Poland) had been added to the list of duty-free products.[17]

During a visit to Washington by Czech President Vaclav Havel in October 1991, the two countries entered into a bilateral agreement on investment that was ratified by the legislatures of the two countries the following year. The pact was a standard bilateral accord that provided that investors from each country would enjoy most favored nation status for their investments; prompt, adequate, and effective compensation in the event of expropriation of an investment; access to international arbitration to settle disputes; and free transfer of capital in a convertible currency.[18] By first quarter 1992, the U.S. Agency for International Development reported that assistance obligations to Czechoslovakia—primarily in the form of technical assistance—totaled $86.5 million. The U.S. State Department concluded that U.S. assistance and progress in negotiating of the investment treaty helped generate about $1.5 billion in direct investment by U.S. companies during late 1991 and early 1992.[19]

With regard to technology transfer to Czechoslovakia and other Eastern European countries, U.S. strategy focused on ways to transfer technology where it bolstered appropriate political and economic reform or enhanced nonproliferation goals. Under this new approach, the United States increasingly directed its efforts toward monitoring the use of technology rather than prohibiting its transfer.

In June 1990, COCOM limited the scope of export controls to proscribed East European destinations and moved from a policy of general denial of high technology exports to a policy of assumed approval. Many high technology requests would now receive COCOM's favorable consideration for countries that represented less of a strategic risk, provided they adopted COCOM-approved safeguard regimes to protect imported technology against unauthorized usage or reexport. At that time, COCOM judged the Soviet Union as still constituting a military threat to the West. East European nations (including Czechoslovakia) were not classified as a military threat, but COCOM agreed that the potential for diversion from Eastern Europe to the Soviet Union and certain third world countries remained a concern.

Delegations from the United States and the soon-to-be renamed Czech and Slovak Federal Republic (CSFR) met that summer to discuss relaxing restrictions on dual-use Western exports to the CSFR. The parties concluded a memorandum of understanding in November 1990 whereby the United States agreed to decontrol high technology exports to the CSFR in stages and the CSFR would, in exchange, create and implement its own system of technology controls that met COCOM's goals.[20]

As a result of the negotiations, the United States and COCOM gave the CSFR (and Hungary and Poland) general "favorable consideration" status for the export of controlled dual-use technologies if it implemented an acceptable program of safeguards against diversion of sensitive technology to unacceptable end users. Under the favorable consideration policy, within 30 days of the application COCOM would approve most high-technology exports to legitimate civilian end users in the CSFR.[21] As the CSFR harmonized its dual-use technology controls with the full range of COCOM controls, the country would be completely removed ("deproscribed") from COCOM's list of countries to which exports of controlled technologies are prohibited. The result was CSFR eligibility for the expeditious transfer of the full range of Western high technology exports. COCOM officially ratified "favorable consideration" treatment for the CSFR on February 7, 1991. The June 1991 COCOM meeting continued the trend toward reducing restrictions on technology transfer to the CSFR, reflecting its entrance into strategic trade agreements with the West to prevent all illegal tampering with Western-supplied technology. However, until it demonstrated a capability to control indigenously produced advanced goods and technologies, that is, military and militarily important items,[22] COCOM would subject the CSFR to a "special procedure" that established a presumption of approval for all but the most sensitive equipment rather than full deproscription.

Although the changes approved for the CSFR during the 1990–92 period were not as dramatic as full deproscription, they alleviated much of the export licensing burden for U.S. high technology companies with extensive operations or sales there. Perhaps most significant in the change of status was the elimination of U.S. Defense Department and COCOM review for export license applications to the CSFR. As a result, exporters could receive an export license from the U.S. Commerce Department in a matter of a few days to a few weeks.[23]

In a related technology transfer policy change, President Bush lifted the long standing U.S. arms embargo against the CSFR. The decision allowed the CSFR to buy "defense articles and services" from the United States under the Foreign Assistance Act of 1961, which originally prohibited such sales.[24] Czechoslovak Defense Minister Lubos Dobrovsky described the decision as very hopeful because imports of certain technologies should enable the speedier conversion of production in CSFR arms plants.[25] The agreement opened the way for improved defense cooperation between the United States and the CSFR.[26]

U.S. Policy Goals and Preferences

The United States pursued several goals through its incentive policies. Some of these goals were quite specific. For example, the creation of an internal licensing and export control apparatus that could regulate the disposition and prohibit the undesired retransfer of Western technology imported by the CSFR was an explicit requirement for the liberalization of U.S. and Western technology transfer restrictions. The United States and COCOM countries also wanted safeguards created to prohibit unauthorized export of indigenous CSFR technology.[27] Relatedly, the United States looked for cooperation in Western efforts to strengthen emerging nonproliferation export control regimes.

Beyond these specific expectations, the United States also hoped the new nation would exercise restraint in making conventional arms sales (a major CSFR export) to countries or areas of instability. In the Middle East, South Asia, and the Balkans, in particular, the United States wished to control the growth in regional arsenals. To reduce the oversupply of arms, the United States expected the conversion of much of the CSFR arms industry to civilian production. Finally, the United States wanted to see the CSFR continue on the path of democratization, free market reform, and reintegration into the world economy—of which conversion of its armaments industries was an important step.[28]

Changing Preferences in the Recipient State

In Czechoslovakia, the "velvet" revolution at the end of 1989 toppled one of the staunchest of communist regimes and replaced it with a new government dedicated to the principles of democracy and market economics. As part of its efforts to integrate politically and economically with the West, the new government, led by former dissident playwright Vaclav Havel, outlined a plan of decentralizing the economy, freeing its currency, and restoring private property.

Czechoslovakia held free elections on June 8, 1990. The Civic Forum, an opposition group to communist rule formed at the end of 1989, and its Slovak counterpart, Public Against Violence, won an impressive parliamentary victory over the Communist party (securing 168 seats out of 300 in the Federal Assembly while the communists captured only 47).[29] Havel was promptly reelected president by the new Federal Assembly. The convincing win gave the reformers a strong mandate to move the country toward democracy and a free-market economy.[30] In November 1990, the republics, Czech and Slovak, signed a power-sharing agreement with the central government that transferred considerable power to them and renamed the country the Czech and Slovak Federal Republic.[31]

Becoming part of Western society and gaining access to Western goods, markets, and technology became explicit goals of the new nation. The postcommunist government saw access to modern Western technology in telecommunications, computers, machine tools, and other sectors as essential to its ability to eventually compete in the global economy. It lacked the capacity to foster any substantial progress from within because of its substantial economic challenges and a legacy of technological backwardness. As Richard Cupitt writes:

> Without a host of modern technologies then subject to COCOM controls . . . the CSFR would be unable to compete effectively in the global economy. Inefficient or uncompetitive industries could not attract foreign investment, placing the burden of conversion squarely on the government and a small coterie of domestic entrepreneurs. There was widespread recognition that modernizing the economy required greater access to Western technology.[32]

Four decades of Western economic and technological sanctions and its economic orientation toward the East had left Czechoslovakia, like many Eastern European countries, technologically antiquated and economically inefficient. After the failed reforms of 1968, Czechoslovakia, unlike Hungary or even Poland, rarely engaged in experiments in market economics. In key technologies, such as telecommunications, Czechoslovakia was literally decades behind the West. Despite its status as one of the most stable and industrialized countries in Europe before World War II, its industrial base was obsolete and overly centralized. Furthermore, Czechoslovakia was not well integrated into global markets. In addition to inadequate telecommunications and transportation facilities, the Czech economy was dependent on trade with the Soviet Union.[33] As in the China case, the recipient's utility for the incentive was strongly positive.

The CSFR made important progress in terms of new legislation, macroeconomic stabilization, and privatization during 1990–92,[34] but at an immediate cost of falling real wages and living standards for many—especially those in the Slovak Republic.[35] The planned reforms—privatization, investment, stabilization, and industrial restructuring—all depended in significant part on participation by foreign investors, the bearers of modern technology, managerial know-how, and capital.[36]

Independent analyses of the Czechoslovak economy confirmed the difficult, but ultimately rewarding, road chosen by the country's leaders. The first economic survey of Czechoslovakia by the Organization for Economic Cooperation and Development, for example, gave the country a glowing review for making rapid progress toward a market economy. The report cited numerous achievements: almost complete liberalization of prices and foreign trade, large subsidy cuts, introduction of key elements of a legal framework for private sector development, laying the groundwork for widespread privatization by vouchers, a sound monetary policy, and an apparent willingness of the population to accept a steep real-wage drop in early 1991. The report added that the CSFR would have to rely on sustained export growth to support its structural transformation.[37]

Obtaining access to the West's resources and markets essential for modernization required incurring certain obligations, however, including cooperation with the West on nonproliferation export controls. In addition to the economic benefits, cooperation with the United States and the West in this area carried symbolic significance for all parties—a clear-cut example of the end of Cold War technological isolation and a symbol of the CSFR's reintegration with, and acceptance by, the West.[38] James F. Brown summarized the prevailing attitude among many in the Czech Republic: "I think that in 1989 and shortly after 1989, nowhere in the world was the stock, the prestige, of the United States as high as it was in Eastern Europe, [there was] this tremendous reservoir of good will and opportunity—political, economic, and cultural opportunity. . . ."[39] Czechoslovak officials sought to convince the West of their government's new approach to East-West relations and raise Czechoslovakia's moral standing.[40]

To qualify for Western technology, the CSFR created a new export control apparatus.[41] Despite the organizational, legal, technical, and economic challenges associated with creating this new governmental function, a broad consensus existed within the new government over the need for such controls. The CSFR quickly implemented controls on imported advanced technology by passing legislation empowering the Federal Foreign Trade Ministry to license the import and export of controlled goods and giving the Customs Administration authority to inspect for compliance with the law and identify violators.[42] A separate law created criminal penalties and punishment for violations.[43] The two provisions created the initial framework for compliance with Western demands for a technology control system.

In addition to addressing COCOM's immediate concerns for control over the proliferation of strategic dual-use technology, the CSFR continued its support for other multilateral export control arrangements. The CSFR signed the "Declaration of the CSCE (Conference on Security and Cooperation in Europe) Council on Nonproliferation and Arms Transfers," promising to prevent the proliferation of weapons of mass destruction and delivery systems. It renewed its support for a comprehensive chemical weapons convention to be concluded in 1992.[44] The CSFR adopted the list of chemical export restrictions of the Australia Group and in November 1990 removed any objection it had to the ban on chemical weapons in the proposed Convention on Chemical and Biological Weapons then under negotiation in Geneva.[45] In the area of nuclear-related exports, the new federation committed itself to the strict guidelines of the Nuclear Suppliers Group, an organization that Czechoslovakia had joined in an earlier incarnation in 1978[46] and became a proponent of a global nuclear test ban.[47] In conventional arms, the CSFR joined the United Nations embargo on Iraq and European Community restrictions applied to Yugoslavia.[48] The federation also approved a CSCE agreement on the maximum levels of conventional weapons and technology in the former Warsaw Pact countries.[49]

Despite these considerable cooperative efforts, the CSFR faced many obstacles in meeting expectations (both its own and the West's) for limitations on arms exports and defense industry conversion. Unlike with dual-use technology exports, the CSFR government was unable to pass legislation controlling arms licensing and exporting.[50] Instead, interagency and interrepublic disputes left arms sales and licensing to a case-by-case process. Despite U.S. encouragement to have CSFR arms export policies conform to COCOM munitions lists, and statements of CSFR good intentions, actual policy in this area was strongly influenced by economic necessity and particular interests.

Obstacles to CSFR Cooperation in Arms Sales and Defense Conversion

The CSFR's process of bureaucratic implementation of technology licensing complicated efforts to cooperate fully with the West. The Foreign Trade Ministry generally supported the granting of export licenses along with the Ministry of Defense (which had an interest in maintaining the defense industry of the CSFR through exports). These views were often contested by the Ministry of Foreign Affairs, which advocated stricter controls over the export of arms, in part because of its greater concern over external relations with the West.[51] The process of removing government control over the economy and the consequent burgeoning number of companies involved in arms trade also complicated arms sale restraint.[52] Relatedly, the development of a powerful arms lobby that included weapons producers, factory managers, and private dealers impeded the ability of the federal legislature to fashion a more coherent arms policy.[53] In short, domestic adjustment costs slowed cooperation appreciably.

In addition to interministerial wrangling over policy implementation, a major hindrance to adopting and implementing new arms export control policies arose from growing interrepublic differences. Under its new government, the federal state granted substantial authority over the economic sphere to the Czech and Slovak Republics. One immediate result of this power dispersion was the Slovak Republic's decision to adopt a different posture regarding arms exports and slow the pace of the federal government's radical defense conversion plans.

Higher levels of unemployment, concentrated defense production, rigid labor markets, uncompetitive industries, inability to absorb advanced technology, greater suspicion of the West, and reemerging nationalism all made the Slovak Republic less cooperative with Western demands for arms sales restraint and defense industry conversion. Growing support for Slovakian independence in 1992 and local interest in maintaining arms exports constrained the negotiating position of the CSFR in dealing with Western demands for restraints on arms sales and defense industry conversion.

Recall that Czechoslovakia, a small country of 15 million citizens, had a long tradition of arms manufacturing and export. Under communist rule, Czechoslovakia devoted more than one-third of its investment in manufacturing to building its defense industry. The majority of government armament investment was in the Slovakian region, particularly in the heavy machine works (tank and armored vehicle production) in the city of Martin and its vicinity.[54]

The collapse of communism and the worldwide decline in the arms market devastated CSFR arms exports. Sales of defense products fell from $1.4 billion in 1987 to $186 million in 1991.[55] This radical drop in sales was reflected in a sudden jump in unemployment. By 1991, the defense industry had lost 30,000 jobs,[56] with 80,000 more jobs at risk, the majority of them in the depressed and restive Slovak Republic.[57]

One possible solution to the economic dislocation associated with declining arms markets is defense industry conversion, that is, the conversion of plants manufacturing and exporting tanks, armored vehicles, and military aircraft to civilian production such as trucks, agricultural and industrial equipment, or civil avionics. The leaders of Czechoslovakia's velvet revolution anticipated, and the West hoped, that the rapid conversion of the arms industry to civilian production would be a mainstay of the new government. Instead, arms industry conversion quickly became a "Czech-versus-Slovak issue."[58] Federal government officials concerned with Czechoslovakia's standing in the West favored rapid conversion,[59] whereas Slovak politicians emphasized the economic hardships that rapid conversion would inflict on their region and that Slovakia's economy should not be sacrificed as part of a "gesture of cooperation to the West."[60] The attempt to straddle these diverse regional perspectives partially explains the inconsistencies that characterized Czech arms sales and conversion policies in 1991 and 1992[61] and contributed to tensions in the CSFR's relations with the United States and the West.

Another factor complicating Czech and Slovak cooperation with the West on arms sales and conversion was the declining importance of greater access to Western technology as a factor in shaping policy by the end of 1992. Having secured favorable consideration status for Western exports from COCOM countries, enterprises in the CSFR had access to all but the most technologically sophisticated items. Most CSFR enterprises, especially those in the Slovak Republic, had little interest in obtaining access to cutting-edge technologies they could neither absorb nor afford. Moreover, U.S. assistance was limited largely to encouraging private-sector participation in the CSFR, rather than making large, official financial transfers as many in the CSFR anticipated.[62] Meciar captured the sentiment well: "The federal government understood conversion as a gesture of cooperation toward the West. They hoped there'd be a payoff, but they're still waiting."[63]

Conclusion

Generally, the CSFR was cooperative or in harmony with the United States and the West. It established an internal technology control system, continued and expanded policies to support weapon nonproliferation, restrained some of its arms sales, and continued on an uneven path of defense conversion. Moreover, the level of cooperation might have been greater had the United States and the West been willing to commit greater financial resources to the CSFR in making its demands or had the West exercised greater restraint in making arms sales itself.[64]

Western incentives were an important factor in shaping some of these policies (particularly the establishment of an internal technology control system) because the United States conditioned receipt of goods and technology critical for the CSFR's economic development on cooperation with COCOM and other multilateral proliferation control regimes. Failure to comply could mean the loss of necessary technology capital and markets.

CSFR cooperation was also shaped by its desire to adopt Western norms and a decline in the international arms market. For example, the West's creation of multilateral nonproliferation export control systems made it easier for the CSFR to enact its own system of technology controls. When explaining their export control, arms, and trade policy, CSFR officials often referenced their international obligations, including adherence to multilateral export control arrangements. CSFR leaders also used international standards and rules as a political tool in building a domestic consensus to support domestic export controls.[65] In arms sales, the collapse of the Warsaw Treaty Organization and declining defense budgets in the West helped constrain the CSFR export practices in keeping with Western aspirations.

The incentive policy was not an unqualified success, however. American influence was limited by several factors, including the split between the two republics, economic dislocation associated with the movement to a free-market economy, and problems of CSFR bureaucratic coordination.

CHAPTER 6

Trade and Technology Incentives and Foreign Policy

This book argues that trade and technology incentives merit attention as a tool for influencing a state's decision on cooperation or noncooperation. It seeks to provide a set of logically consistent hypotheses on how incentives work in bilateral relations. A better theoretical understanding of economic incentives may be useful knowledge to foreign policymakers because it can provide general insights helpful in determining the viability of an incentive strategy in present and future contexts. These insights are needed because, while scholars have given insufficient attention to developing a theory of economic incentives, policymakers have nonetheless employed incentive strategies (as the case studies illustrate), and (as noted in the introduction chapter) their enthusiasm for such strategies is growing.

The purpose of this chapter is to draw on the theoretical insights of chapter 2 and to extract generalizations from the case studies to suggest some of the factors policymakers should consider in deciding to use or not use economic incentives. It attempts to answer the questions: When do economic incentives work best, and what factors contribute to, or detract from, their success in fostering bilateral cooperation?

What Contribution Can Scholarship Make to Policy-making?

Foreign policymakers face the challenge of pursuing national interests and managing relationships with other states in the international system. In a recent work, Alexander George summarizes the myriad tasks that face the policymaker:

> Policymakers [must] clearly define their own state's interests, differentiate these interests in terms of relative importance, and make prudent judgments as to acceptable costs and risks of pursuing them. . . . Policymakers must identify, analyze, and deal with conflicts of interest

with other states. When an accommodation of their conflicting interests is not possible, policymakers must try to narrow and manage the disputed issues in ways that reduce the potential for destructive conflicts and contamination of the entire relationship. At the same time, the development and management of relationships with other states requires leaders to recognize and seek out common interests and develop policies for promoting them. Statecraft includes strategies for cooperation . . . as well as conflict avoidance, management, and resolution.[1]

Needless to say, the knowledge base required for these difficult tasks is immense, and much of it lies outside the province of international relations theory. Moreover, as George reminds us, theoretical knowledge is an aid to, not a substitute for, policy-making judgments that must be made in the context of a particular situation.

Still, policymakers can benefit from scholarship. George identifies three research products of scholarship that are useful to policy judgments: (1) a conceptual framework for different strategies and instruments available to policymakers seeking to influence other states; (2) "generic knowledge" of each strategy, which identifies its uses, limitations, and the conditions required to effectively implement the strategy; and (3) actor-specific models of adversaries' behavior.[2] This study can contribute to the first two types of policy-relevant knowledge and identify areas where the third is especially useful.

A quasi-deductive theory of a particular strategy (in this case, trade and technology incentives) should, according to George, identify the critical variables of that strategy and the general logic associated with successful use of that policy instrument.[3] These models, like the one presented in chapter 2, are a starting point for understanding the basic prerequisites for, and logic behind, the implementation of a particular strategy. Although international relations theory is not of the scientific quality that would permit one to predict whether a strategy would succeed or fail in every situation, empirical research that systematically examines the use of a strategy in past cases can compensate for this weakness by identifying for policymakers conditions that favor (or impede) successful operation of a strategy. These conditional generalizations are what George calls "generic knowledge."

Although the task of identifying numerous important conditions, or "variables," runs contrary to the theorist's search for parsimony, wrestling with such complexities and ambiguities is a way of life for policymakers. By identifying some of the conditions important to the success or failure of a strategy as suggested by case studies, the scholar can help the policymaker assemble a checklist for use in assessing the feasibility or desirability of that strategy in the policymaker's present situation. That list will be useful to the policymaker even if the conclusions are merely plausible (rather than scientifically certain) and the analysis from which it is compiled is complex or "rich" (rather than parsimonious).[4] This chapter concludes with a preliminary list of necessary and favoring conditions for the success of an incentive strategy.

Economic Incentives as a Foreign Policy Strategy: Necessary and Favoring Conditions for Success

Chapter 2 offers a two-level exchange model. The model demonstrates the importance of considering how a proposed incentive might change the payoff structure facing a recipient and how the proposed incentive interacts with domestic political factors in the policymaker's home state and in the recipient state.

As to the international payoff structure, incentives require the existence of, or potential for, a bilateral exchange relationship. Further, the relationship must be one in which the policymaker's country has in some way impeded the full recognition of trade gains available to the potential recipient (such as an embargo, tariff or nontariff barrier, capital restriction, or other impediment) or has used policies to obtain preferable terms of trade. Political influence comes by forgoing trade gains for a change in the recipient's political behavior. If market forces alone set the terms, then the sender has nothing to offer. Existing impediments to maximizing trade gains or shifting trade terms in favor of a party are ubiquitous features of international relations. Further, unlike sanctions, monopoly power or asymmetrical dominance by the sender are not required.

For an incentive strategy to succeed, the international market must be characterized by a sender who values the political concession more highly than the recipient does. The incentive must be introduced into or create a situation in which the two states (sender and recipient) possess different preference functions. That is, for the exchange to occur, the recipient state must value the potential economic benefit more highly than the political concession demanded of it, and the sender must value the political concession more highly than the material benefit it must forgo. This is the definition of a successful influence attempt. As demonstrated in the China case, these conditions do not preclude the sender from also benefiting through expanded commercial exchange, nor do they preclude the recipient state from extracting certain political advantages from its cooperative adjustment. These conditions only indicate that the parties weigh the value of the fundamental trade-off differently.

In addition to the existence of an economic market, the case studies suggest a second potentially necessary condition, the existence of a minimum degree of trust or confidence in the bilateral relationship. Just as an economic market between the parties is necessary, a "political market" for exchange is necessary, too. Buyers and sellers must be certain of the creditworthiness of parties to a transaction and that offers and conditions for fulfillment of promises will be understood by all. Before a deal can be struck, the parties must have a degree of confidence that the party with whom they are dealing understands them and understands the quid pro quo of the incentive. As Thomas Schelling notes, "Expectations have to be constructed out of successful experience, not all at once, out of intentions."[5] In relationships characterized by an atmosphere of hostility, mistrust, and misunderstanding, ambitious incentives may be a premature, if not dangerous, policy choice. In popular parlance, confidence-building measures designed to change perceptions of hostile intent may be necessary before a programmatic incentive is possible or warranted.[6]

The China case study helps illustrate this point. Significant cooperation became possible only as the threat of China to the United States diminished and a reasonable basis existed to conclude that China sought improved relations with the United States and vice versa. The evolution of cooperation in that case is an important point. The two countries built cooperation in stages, beginning with modest cultural exchange, expanding to limited economic rapprochement and recognition, and culminating in substantial economic incentives and a measure of political and strategic cooperation. Once established, cooperation between the two countries remained relatively strong despite growing divergences in their strategic orientations. Even when the anti-Soviet rationale for cooperation had waned for China, the economic foundation of cooperation endured. This process of laying the foundation for a meaningful incentive strategy took nearly a decade (a short period by Chinese foreign policy standards, an exceedingly long one by American standards). The case of incentives offered to the Czech and Slovak Federal Republic (CSFR) involved a much shorter time period of confidence building and ripening, perhaps as a result of the extraordinary and rapid disintegration of the Warsaw Pact. In both cases, a clearly communicated desire by both parties for a different relationship was a prerequisite to a more ambitious attempt at cooperation. Likewise, the bilateral agreement between the United States and Sweden was part of a larger initiative launched several years earlier, and the period of civilian nuclear cooperation lasted more than a decade.

The time needed to lay the foundation for a successful incentive strategy may be a luxury unavailable to policymakers in every instance. Still, hasty incentive strategies may be worse than no incentive strategy at all.

Incentives may be inappropriate policy instruments in an atmosphere of mistrust and misunderstanding that makes the incentive effort likely to be misconstrued or in the presence of an immediate danger posed by the recipient's pursuit of noncooperative actions. Although a thorough study is not attempted here, U.S.-Iraq relations before the Gulf War may illustrate the point. If Iraq were acquiring weapons and frightening its neighbors in the search for its security, then a long-term incentive that enhanced Iraq's security, while clearly indicating the policy adjustment for which the incentives were offered, could have been an appropriate strategy in moderating behavior in a more cooperative direction. If, as was more likely the case, Iraq was acquiring weapons and behaving in a bellicose fashion because it was hell-bent on aggressive military action against its neighbors, then hastily assembled incentives that had not established a dialogue between the sender and recipient, especially those without defined conditions, may have been a foolhardy policy instrument, at least until steps were taken to halt the immediate threat and a foundation for cooperative influence had been established. If little basis to communicate anticipated cooperative adjustment or the imminent danger exists, then threats or punishments may be the only viable option in the short run.

Finally, incentives require protracted implementation and hence necessitate some degree of institutional capability in the sender state. Incentives, if accepted by the recipient in the sense that the recipient indicates a likelihood of cooperating, require action and implementation by the sender. This feature contrasts to sanctions, which require implementation when the recipient indicates an intention *not* to adapt its policies in the direction desired by the sender.[7] The burden of implementation means that an effective incentive policy requires bureaucratic coordination and follow-through and, while most advanced states possess this institutional capability, its effective use cannot be assumed.

For example, problems of implementation characterized the U.S. decision to liberalize technology transfer to the People's Republic of China (PRC) in the early and mid-1980s. By the end of 1982, President Reagan's "two-times" decision (doubling the level of sophistication of permissible technology exports to China) had bogged down in the U.S. bureaucracy and drawn the ire of the PRC government and the U.S. exporting community. Chinese officials voiced displeasure over U.S. licensing policy and practice. In 1983, Huang Hua, the former foreign minister of the PRC, told the Council on Foreign Relations, "In view of the recent developments . . . one cannot help but ask, 'Does the United States view China as a friend or foe?'"[8] During a spring 1983 visit to the PRC, Secretary of State George Schultz heard similar concerns expressed by Deng Xiaoping, who described U.S. technology transfer policy as "capricious."[9] In summing up Chinese frustrations with the problems of U.S. bureaucratic implementation, one Chinese official said the policies had "led to much thunder, little rain."[10] Likewise, U.S. exporters charged in the early 1980s that U.S. technology licensing policy toward the PRC remained equivocal and inefficient and unnecessarily impeded the transfer of technology. They attributed part of the delay and confusion to the interagency license review process and the lack of cooperation between agencies, particularly the Departments of Commerce and Defense in ruling on license applications.[11] The Defense Department adopted a more negative stance on rendering licensing approval, as one might expect given its bureaucratic mission.[12] Although these problems were ameliorated and did not fundamentally undermine the initiative, the problem of bureaucratic implementation and interagency coordination remained an impediment to a more effective incentive policy. In short, an incentive strategy requires that the bureaus charged with its implementation have the capability, the legislative or executive oversight, and their own incentives to see that the policy is substantially effected.

Likewise, some degree of institutional strength and state power is important to implement the recipient's cooperative change sought by the sender. That is, the recipient state must have some corresponding institutional capability to respond effectively to an incentive. The weakness of the CSFR's legal and bureaucratic apparatus, for example, hindered cooperation in staunching arms exports. This observation implies that incentives may not be appropriate for dealing with very weak states, revolutionary states, and nonstate actors that may encounter insurmountable difficulty in implementing cooperative intentions.

Other factors or conditions contribute to, or detract from, the success of economic incentives. At the level of international exchange, market power is an important condition favoring the success of an incentive. Unlike economic coercion strategies, however, market power is not a strict necessity. More market power in the incentive goods is better than less because it creates a larger potential economic benefit that can be exchanged for the desired political concession. In this sense, incentive power may be more relevant to economically powerful or technologically sophisticated states. However, a sender state does not need to exercise monopoly power in a good or technology to exercise influence. As noted in chapter 2, unlike sanctions, third-party entrants are unlikely to be a significant problem in incentive strategies. Therefore, any gainful exchange relationship (or the potential for one) and any governmental policy that affects the distribution of the gains from trade in favor of itself create a potential avenue for political influence.

In light of this point, one could argue that although the focus here has been on the United States as the sender state, incentives may be equally or more important policy instruments for other countries. The United States as a military superpower and a leading nation in many multilateral forums has a wide range of policy instruments available to it, in addition to economic incentives. Other countries, whose policy alternatives may be less extensive, that for practical or historical reasons have strict limitations on their military statecraft, or that lack the market power to make sanctions stick, might have greater interest in using economic incentives to achieve more cooperative foreign relations over time. Arguably, even the United States, whose relative power position has receded from post–World War II heights, may find incentives an increasingly attractive alternative. To the extent international interdependence reduces the efficacy or raises the costs of military measures, all states may find incentives a more attractive option.

In choosing an incentive policy, it is necessary to understand the economic and political aspirations of the potential recipient. To what degree does the potential recipient value the incentive goods, capital, or technology? How are those material aspirations linked to fundamental state interests in economic growth, prosperity, and political legitimacy and stability? The incentive is more likely to be influential if the recipient state highly values the incentive and if acquisition of the incentive is linked to abiding state interests (political and economic).

All three cases reflect a strong desire for the incentive in the potential recipient and a strong instrumental link between trade and technology and recipient state aspirations. China, for example, had clearly identified a developmental model that emphasized the need to acquire modern technology. China also indicated that greater prosperity (and a period of more cooperative international relations that would facilitate economic growth) was its fundamental national strategy for the remainder of the twentieth century. Understanding the importance China attached to trade and technology as part of its modernization effort helped the United States fashion an incentive strategy and allowed it to define, to a degree, the direction of Chinese cooperative adaptation. As discussed in chapter 5, reintegration with the West and modernization of its economic infrastructure were paramount political/symbolic and economic goals of the new CSFR. Given the importance of Western trade, technology, and capital to its future, the country was generally receptive to the U.S. incentive strategy. In the case of Sweden, the opposite was true. The ruling Social Democrats linked their prestige to greater energy self-sufficiency, technological self-reliance, and neutrality. These political and economic aspirations and intentions initially reduced their desire for American light water technology and impeded Sweden's willingness to abandon an objective (the bomb project) that was linked to these goals.

It is true that the utility a recipient attaches to an incentive declines with additional units of the good or technology. For example, the attractiveness of Western high technology for the CSFR waned somewhat as the country's ability to absorb the incentive was reached. Nonetheless, to the extent the recipient continues to attach significant positive value to the incentive, that is, as long as total utility is rising, incentives may be powerful tools of influence. Technology, which has a pervasive and enduring role in states' output, is likely to be valued highly by recipients over the long term.

One potential pitfall of this analysis should be noted. In estimating the utility a potential recipient will place on an economic incentive, the sender state should not substitute or project its values as a substitute for knowledge of the potential recipient's values. This situation might be called the "mirror image" problem in policy-making. Just as assuming rationality may be unwarranted in anticipating policy responses, it is also incorrect to assume that a recipient state will value incentives much like one's own state would. This fallacy was one of the problems that beset U.S. restrictions on technology toward the Soviet Union during the Cold War. When American policymakers confronted the task of determining which technologies had potential military utility for the Soviets and should be denied export, they often made their judgments based on the proxy of what dual-use technology was important to *American* military systems. CIA studies during the 1980s documented that the mirror image approach was often misleading and led to restrictions on the wrong technologies.[13] Indeed, the effectiveness of incentives requires that the recipient value the economic incentive more highly than sender does relative to the political concession. Given this necessary condition, estimating the value of the incentive for the recipient through actor-specific knowledge is an important determination.

Policymakers must also consider domestic conditions in weighing the possible employment of an incentive strategy. Incorporating domestic politics into the model is an advantage of the two-level model of incentives. With regard to conditions in the sender state, every policymaker is acutely aware that effective policies must be sold within his or her government and, to the extent the issue is of importance to particular groups and the electorate, supported by the domestic society. The case studies are particularly useful in helping identify some important factors to consider in this respect.

With regard to the domestic society of the sender state, policymakers should recognize that incentives, by opening or expanding trade and exchange relations, are virtually certain to create potential partners among affected interest groups in the domestic society who are motivated to see the incentive work. This effect is in contrast to economic sanctions, which, by interrupting trade, necessarily create dissension among adversely impacted groups. In the case of civilian nuclear technology incentives offered to Sweden, the chief societal partner was the emerging nuclear reactor industry headed by industrial giants like General Electric and Westinghouse. In the other two cases, a wide spectrum of medium and high technology American exporters stood to gain by an incentive policy that would open an important new market and investment opportunity. Incentive strategies can also raise opposition from domestic groups whose economic or political interests are adversely affected by increased commercial exchange. Typically, those industries or labor groups in sectors that face adjustment costs by virtue of greater openness in international trade and technology transfer may oppose an incentive policy or demand a side payment. For example, although the American consumer and market sectors that purchased material and components from the PRC benefited by the normalization of trade relations, American textile manufactures were chagrined to see the American market open to China. Political objections to the incentive strategy may also arise. Some American human rights organizations voiced concern or opposition to liberalizing economic relations with the PRC for noneconomic reasons, for instance. As a general point, policymakers should recognize that incentives are more successful when domestic partners can be identified and mobilized in support of the strategy and societal groups that are actually or potentially adverse to the policy can be compensated materially or placated politically.

Orchestrating domestic support for a new policy direction is always difficult, but incentives may be an easier policy instrument behind which to rally a winning domestic coalition than other economic instruments. As noted in chapter 2, unlike more costly policies, incentives may require less appeal to patriotic principles to extract the necessary sacrifice from adversely affected groups in the domestic society, yet, because they have an overtly political purpose, policymakers can more credibly invoke ideals such as global peace or national security to garner support for the incentive strategy. The cases suggest that gaining widespread public support for an incentive strategy may be less of a concern than contending with the balancing of particular domestic interests. Incentives, unlike sanctions, raise few fears or concerns in the sender state's populace of escalating international tensions. All the incentive programs examined carried a positive message of offering tangible benefits to others in pursuit of an important national interest and greater international cooperation. Whether the bilateral cooperation achieved in any of these instances actually contributed to greater global peace and prosperity is a separate matter. What the cases suggest is that idealistic messages associated with incentive policies can help generate widespread public sentiment in favor of the policies. Generally, incentives work well for the sender to the extent they can be promulgated to appeal beyond narrow economic or political gain to broadly held ideals or aspirations. As discussed subsequently, this favoring condition may be an impediment to the policy's success to the extent that keeping an incentive policy quiet permits the recipient greater freedom to accommodate the sender's wishes without creating impressions in *its* domestic society that it is capitulating to foreign influence.

Domestic conditions favoring or disfavoring successful operation of incentives in the recipient state are likewise critically important considerations for policymakers. Chapter 2 suggests that one of the reasons incentives may work better than a model focused exclusively on the international payoff structure is the interaction between incentives and the recipient state. Incentives create partners in the recipient state who favor execution of the incentive policy and will therefore exert pressure in the recipient state for the desired political adaptation, whereas sanctions are more certain to create groups with a vested interest in seeing the sanction continue and cooperation resisted. Policymakers should identify those groups in the recipient state that have an economic or political stake in the acceptance, continuation, or expansion of an economic incentive. The policymaker should ask, "Who in the recipient state will appropriate the gains from exchange and how can they influence the actions of the recipient state? Who in the recipient state has a political stake in seeing the desired policy adaptation?" These allies may be private groups—the civilian power industry in Sweden that sought the latest and cheapest technology and nuclear fuel, for example—or state actors—such as modernizers in China or political and economic liberals in the CSFR. In general, incentives work better when important allies in the recipient state help sell the desired policy adaptation to, or within, the recipient state government. Like the situation in the sender state, incentives are less likely to work when the desired policy adaptation generates strong opposition among groups for economic and political reasons. Perhaps the clearest example of this latter phenomenon was the opposition of the Slovak arms industry to rapid conversion and a ban on arms exports, policies initially championed by the reform-minded government of the CSFR.

State strength vis-à-vis society may be an important consideration. A strong state, like the PRC, may be able to overcome domestic malcontents in choosing cooperation and is more likely to be able to follow through with cooperative adjustment if it adopts that path. A weak state, like the CSFR, was held hostage, to some extent, by minority interests opposed to cooperation (i.e., Slovak arms manufacturers and regional politicians). On the other hand, strong states drive tough bargains. An example would be China's ability to pressure the United States to make good on its economic promises and its ability to resist being pushed too far politically. Conceivably, a weak state might be more susceptible to foreign pressures, especially if exercised in tandem with a powerful domestic interest group.

The cases are not sufficient to make a strong statement here, but they suggest that the most propitious state-society balance for effective influence may turn on whether the chief ally in the recipient state is situated within the government or society. When the important allies are within the state, a strong recipient state is preferable. In the case of the CSFR, the most important supporter of the incentive strategy was probably the liberal, Western-oriented leaders in the government. Hence, a stronger, more established state could have improved cooperative adjustment in that case. In contrast, when the chief ally is in the society, a more "penetrable" state is preferable. For example, the chief booster of the American incentives in Sweden came to be the domestic electrical power industry, which, while important in Swedish politics, could not overcome the government's protracted opposition to a light water nuclear strategy until a host of other forces within the government and in the external environment had made adopting that strategy a possibility.

As alluded to earlier, in deciding how much visibility to give to an incentive strategy, policymakers should consider the role of public opinion and the need for public support for cooperative adjustment in the recipient state. In some cases, it may be necessary to balance the need for publicity at home against the recipient state's need for discretion. In certain situations, casting cooperative adjustment as harmony ("We are acting only in the interest of China, not in response to foreign pressure") may be beneficial for the recipient government's image. Alternatively, acknowledging cooperative adaptation in response to an incentive may carry important symbolic value that the recipient can use to bolster its domestic legitimacy. As discussed in chapter 5, the new CSFR government craved recognition and acceptance by the West and was not adverse to the image that it was paying the political dues necessary to join the club. Generally, incentives may work best when both the sender and the recipient can use the policy for public propaganda purposes or to bolster its self-image.

Chapter 2 also hypothesizes as to the superior communication potential of incentives relative to sanctions. Policymakers should make the most of this function by delivering a message of desired policy adaptation. It may be advantageous to make the desired adaptation quite specific, for example, the requirement that the CSFR develop a minimally acceptable level of internal controls on imported technology, or more diffuse, for example, the desire to see arms sales restrained or the desire for Chinese cooperation across a broad spectrum of political and strategic issues. The cases are too few to suggest when demands should be more specific or more diffuse, but because incentives can give a precise and nonthreatening signal of the desired policy adaptation, the sender should be clear or purposeful in delivering its message.[14] Again, the U.S.-Iraq situation before the Gulf War, although not examined in this study, may illustrate the danger of incentive policy where the sender had muddled or ignored the communication function of incentives.

The cases in this book also alert us to the fact that incentives can communicate powerfully to third parties as well as to intended recipients. The cases suggest that this collateral communication was, and should be, considered by policymakers in fashioning an incentive strategy. As noted, one of the goals of the U.S. bilateral agreements for cooperation in civilian nuclear technology was to communicate to the nonaligned world the benefits of closer relations with the United States and to demonstrate to the Soviet Union a willingness to compete for international influence. The China case presents an even more dramatic case of third-party messages. American incentives heightened Soviet suspicions of the United States and carried a threatening message to the USSR that was part of an increased tension in the relationship during the early 1980s. Immediately after the "China tilt" decision in 1980, the Soviets reportedly were quite concerned about the possibility of military cooperation or a tacit alliance between the United States and China. Officially, Prime Minister Aleksei Kosygin, speaking in February 1980, warned that the Soviet Union would give "unremitting attention to the question of defense capability of the U.S.S.R." He added, "No one must be left in any doubt that the U.S.S.R. will not allow any disturbance in the balance of forces which has come about in the world to the detriment of its security."[15] Shortly thereafter, Premier Leonid Brezhnev reiterated Soviet consternation in an interview with former French Prime Minister Jacques Chaban-Delmas, where, accompanied by desk pounding, he shouted, "Believe me, after the destruction of Chinese nuclear sites by our missiles, there won't be much time for the Americans to choose between defense of their Chinese allies and peaceful coexistence."[16] As a general point, policymakers should consider how an incentive policy is introduced into a wider international context and whether it will likely be viewed by third parties positively or negatively. To the extent these collateral communications are consistent with the goals of the sender state, they constitute an auxiliary benefit of the strategy.

A Foreign Policy Checklist

These statements about the conditions favoring the success of an incentive strategy are, admittedly, far from exhaustive and far from certain. Still, they allow us to generate a preliminary checklist for policymakers considering the use of an economic incentive strategy. The *necessary conditions* for the successful (cooperation-inducing) use of an incentive strategy include:

> The existence of, or potential for, a bilateral economic exchange relationship in which sender state policies have limited the full realization of trade gains or where the terms of trade can be shifted in favor of the potential recipient;
>
> The existence of a "political market" between the two parties, where a level of mutual understanding exists or has been built so that neither feels immediately threatened by the other and both have a reasonable expectation that the other will keep its commitments; and
>
> Institutional capability in the sender state to implement the incentive if the decision is made to launch the policy and sufficient stability and institutional strength in the recipient state to assure implementation of cooperation should the recipient state adopt more cooperative policies.

Numerous factors favor the success of an incentive strategy. Some of these favoring conditions exist at the level of international exchange, others depend on conditions in the sender or recipient state. Among the *favoring conditions* suggested by the case studies are the following:

> Systemic Factors
>> Creating new gains from trade or exchange from the incentive policy that can offer economic benefits to both the sender and the recipient states (rather than merely shifting existing terms of trade); and
>> Market power in the incentive goods, services, or technology that creates a larger amount of potential trade gains that can be offered in exchange for political concessions.
>
> Sender State Factors
>> Strong domestic allies in the sender state society who have an economic or political stake in the success of the strategy and are willing to mobilize resources to support the policy;
>> Publicity in the sender state that links the incentive strategy to widely held images and aspirations of society at large, such as

the desire for more cooperative and peaceful international relations or humanitarian values; and

Sender messages regarding the preferred pace and direction for cooperation that are consonant with its desires for specific or diffuse cooperation and third-party messages (for example implying a promise of reward or a warning to parties that are not immediately involved in the transaction) that further auxiliary goals of the sender.

Recipient State Factors

Strong demand for the incentive goods, services, or technology in the recipient state and linkage between acquiring the incentive and fundamental recipient state interests;

Stakeholders in the recipient state who stand to benefit economically and/or politically from the incentive strategy and who are willing and able to exert influence on or within their government to respond with cooperative adaptation; and

Public perceptions in the recipient state that view the incentive as nonthreatening to state sovereignty or national pride and that attach positive symbolic importance to more cooperative relations with the sender as well as appreciating the economic gain to be had.

Success appears less likely when these conditions are not present or when the opposite of these conditions exist. To give an example, an incentive strategy is less likely to succeed when the sender state lacks market power in the goods, services, or technology to be exchanged and the recipient state attaches a relatively low utility to them given its national objectives.

Incentives or Sanctions?

As mentioned in the initial chapter, the literature has generally concluded that economic sanctions rarely produce cooperative policy change in the target because sanctions are costly to the sender in economic and political terms and because they create reactions in the recipient that ameliorate their effect.[17] This book does not take issue with that conclusion. However, when coupled with the assumption that incentives are merely weak sanctions, this conclusion could lead to the erroneous belief that incentives are even less likely to achieve cooperative change in the target's policies. In fact, for the reasons discussed, incentives may have greater potential for cooperative influence than sanctions may.

Moreover, the particular conditions needed for sanctions to work for compellant purposes are quite rigorous and rare, whereas the necessary conditions for a successful incentive policy are more widely available. In the case of sanctions, three strenuous conditions must exist to move the target state in the desired direction. First, the sender needs a near monopoly over trading relations with the target country. If multilateral cooperation is required to achieve that level of market power, the sanction is unlikely to succeed because opposition from any quarter can neutralize the sanction policy. Second, sanctions are only likely to work against targets that are heavily dependent on the sender state for its trade so that the sender can impose substantial costs on the target. The dependency relationship must not only be extensive but asymmetrical as well. The sender cannot be *interdependent* on the target, otherwise economic costs to the sender will be too high for the sanction to succeed. Third, the sender must be capable of implementing the sanction swiftly to affect the target before the rally-around-the-flag and third-party antidotes neutralize its impact. Clearly, the unique market conditions, bilateral relationship, and sender institutional capabilities that must align for sanctions to work optimally in compelling adjustment are uncommon. The conditions require a set of market forces that are increasingly unlikely in an age of multiple centers of economic and technological capabilities. They also make heavy demands on the ability of the sender's domestic political institutions to act with great dispatch while absorbing costs that inevitably will undermine support for the policy.[18]

Although unlikely to produce interstate cooperation, sanctions serve other goals somewhat better. Sanctions are valuable tools to (1) indicate a sender's displeasure, (2) block a target's actions or increase its costs in the short term, (3) satisfy a sender's desire for justice or revenge, (4) demonstrate outrage or resolve to foreign or domestic audiences, and (5) fulfill a political or psychological need to "do something" without incurring the costs associated with military intervention.

However, if cooperation is the goal, then incentives may be a more appropriate—and available—policy instrument. As noted, incentives have several, seldom-considered advantages. Further, incentives do not require the stringent conditions of sanctions to generate some influence in encouraging cooperative policy adjustment.

The Efficacy of Incentives

If the material and political bases for incentive strategy are potentially available in many situations, a policymaker's first question might be: What, generally, is the likelihood of success in using an economic incentive strategy? The cases in this study allow us to respond in a preliminary way to the question of the efficacy of economic incentives. In doing so, however, it is important to remind ourselves of certain basic points about the successful use of policy instruments generally and economic statecraft in particular. First, success in attaining foreign policy objectives is always a matter of degree. As David Baldwin cautions, we should remember that, in statecraft, "Neither perfect success nor perfect failure is likely. Simple dichotomies categorizing outcomes of influence attempts in terms of 'success' or 'failure' can be highly misleading."[19] Second, in reaching determinations of success or failure, it is most useful for the policymaker to think in terms of comparative costs and benefits. A more relevant question for the policymaker is, "How successful are incentives in achieving policy goals given the costs of using incentives as compared to the costs and benefits associated with other available policy options or strategies?"[20]

The theory and the cases presented commend a greater appreciation for the potential efficacy of incentive power. The theory of incentives describes how incentives alter the economic payoff facing states much like sanctions do, but they are easier policies to promote and maintain in the sender state, they do not produce the antidotes in the target state that undermine their effectiveness, and they communicate the path of cooperation more clearly in a manner that the recipient is more likely to perceive accurately. Together, the theory and the case studies caution us to avoid sweeping generalizations about the likely success or failure of economic incentives and encourage us to question the conventional wisdom that economic instruments are unlikely to influence a target and that incentives are particularly unlikely to do so. The bottom line for policymakers is that the beneficial influence of incentives may be underrated, especially when success is defined as cooperative influence and is measured through comparing the costs and benefits of available options.

When a policy instrument's success is measured in cost-benefit terms relative to other instruments and cooperation is the benchmark of success, incentives look even more attractive. All policy choices entail costs. "Choosing economic statecraft—or any other kind of statecraft for that matter—costs something," Baldwin explains.[21] With incentives, the sender state must be willing to forgo its existing economic benefits, or at a minimum not fully exploit or capture new economic benefits for its country alone. This forbearance allows for the exchange of economic benefits from the sender for political concessions from the recipient.

Like most economic instruments, the cost of economic incentives is generally far lower than the cost of military statecraft. Moreover, as discussed in chapter 2, the material costs of incentives may be lower still than the cost of other forms of economic statecraft, such as sanctions. Incentives, unlike sanctions, can create economic gains for both the sender and the recipient rather than necessarily imposing a net economic loss on the sender. In cases where new gains from trade are created, the only "cost" to the sender is the forgone portion of additional gains it might have secured given its market power in the traded goods. This can be seen as a "loss" or cost in one sense, but in absolute terms, trade incentives can be viewed as economically and politically rewarding policy instruments for a sender state. Even when the incentive is more distributional (altering existing terms of trade, for example) or involves a transfer of resources such as foreign aid, the costs may be offset to a degree. A large portion of Marshall Plan aid, for example, returned to the United States in purchases of U.S. goods and services that fueled the American postwar expansion. Countries "tie" aid to purchases of the sender's products, services, and technology precisely to reduce the costs associated with that form of economic incentive.[22] Gain sharing and cost offsetting features of incentives make them "inexpensive" strategies.

In nonmaterial terms, incentives may be less costly (if not gainful) instruments compared to sanctions or military statecraft. Incentives involve the transfer of a material benefit and often carry a powerful positive symbolic message that a sender state can use to bolster its international image. Unlike the exercise of many other forms of power, the sender, recipient, and third parties often perceive them as nonthreatening policy instruments. President Eisenhower's "Atoms for Peace" plan recognized the significant propaganda value that his strategy would have in "winning friends" in the Cold War competition, for example. This nonmaterial "reputational" offset also reduces the costs associated with an incentive strategy.

One qualification regarding cost is in order, however. While in most situations it is advantageous to keep the costs of a policy low relative to performance, this relationship is not always desirous. Some have argued that one of the advantages of sanctions or military measures relative to less costly measures is that they show commitment and resolve through the sender's willingness to incur substantial costs, even if the likelihood of success of the policy is low. Chapter 4 illustrated how the justification for the U.S. embargo of China in the 1960s came to rest on this argument when it became clear that the embargo would not topple the communist government. More often than not, however, policymakers look for strategies that maximize benefits at low cost. This book suggests that economic incentives may possess greater ability to influence the behavior of other states than is generally realized and can do so relatively cheaply. To the extent policymakers seek efficient policies, much commends economic incentives.

Having given a qualified endorsement of incentives as a policy option, this study also supports the argument that one should not overestimate the political concessions or degree of cooperation that can be purchased through economic incentives. Each case demonstrates some limit to cooperative influence. In the case of U.S. civilian nuclear technology incentives to Sweden, this factor was one of many influencing the outcome of events. American incentives conditioned the payoff environment facing Swedish decision makers in a way that favored relinquishing its independent nuclear capabilities needed to produce a bomb. Other external factors were also important. At the agent level, the incentive combined with other forces at play in Swedish domestic policies to influence that country's preferences and choice, but it was not uniquely or solely determinative of the outcome.

The China and CSFR cases reveal another form of limit to incentive power. While China moved closer to the United States in several areas of political and strategic importance, cooperative adjustment was uneven and often contentious, perhaps because of its novel and uninstitutionalized nature or because of systemic constraints. Moreover, as the Tiananmen Square incident demonstrates, China willingly put economic incentives at risk when it determined that fundamental internal stability was at stake. United States and Western economic relations were not sufficient to stop the PRC's leaders from suppressing its own people from alleged foreign ideas when it judged the survival of its regime in peril. Certain political concessions are not for sale. The CSFR case, while less dramatic, makes a similar point: that a political concession may be for sale, but the price may be too high for the sender state. The failure to dissuade the CSFR from making certain military sales where the political and economic advantages of concluding sales overmatched those of incentives designed to encourage the CSFR to forgo them. Interestingly, CSFR politicians often made clear that the scales could have been tipped the other way had the incentive been more substantial. In other words, such a concession had its price, but the sender failed to meet it.

In sum, if the policy goal is punishment, short-run prevention, or demonstration of resolve, then sanctions may be the appropriate choice. Incentives are not well suited for deterring unwanted actions and, when wrongly employed, can be the handmaiden of appeasement. Rather, the cases examined suggest that incentives are reasonable and effective tools for encouraging cooperation over the long term.

CHAPTER 7

Conclusion

This chapter reviews briefly the goals and methods of this study and suggests avenues for future research. The central purpose of this book was narrowly drawn: to develop an explanation of how economic incentives (particularly trade and technology transfer) work in bilateral relations. The study defined *work* to mean the production of a discernible degree of other-regarding policy adjustment in the recipient's actions, that is, cooperation. In addition, the study has sought to generate a set of considerations that would be useful for policymakers to bear in mind in determining the applicability of an incentive strategy to contemporary problems.

Given these goals and limitations on available resources, the method chosen was an intensive, systematic, comparative analysis of a few cases, rather than a broader, statistical analysis of many cases. The approach chosen is more fruitful at this first stage in research on economic incentives where the goal is to generate probabilistic generalizations rather than subject those generalizations to rigorous scrutiny or "testing."[1]

The explanation for the operation of trade and technology incentives in bilateral relations combines the notion of an international exchange of economic benefits for political goods with a set of logically consistent hypotheses on the domestic political economy of incentives. Incentives alter both the international payoff structure facing states and the domestic politics and economics of both the sender and the recipient. Although long overlooked, incentives are not merely weak sanctions but have unique strengths and limitations as tools of statecraft.

Externally, incentives offer an exchange of economic gains from trade and technology transfer for political concessions. Incentives may be compelling in altering state behavior and fostering bilateral cooperation over time, especially when: (1) both the sender and the recipient stand to gain in economic terms through the creation of new trade; (2) the recipient's *total* utility for the goods or gains from trade remains substantially positive (this situation may occur when technology is a part of the package because technology alters a state's overall productive capacity); and (3) the sender has market power in the traded goods. Internally, incentives shape state preferences in a cooperative direction in four important ways, in contrast to sanctions. First, societal actors in the sender state who stand to gain economically from expanded trade lend support over time for an incentive, thereby improving the policy's legitimacy and endurance. Public opinion is likely to follow the lead of elites. Second, certain actors in the recipient state who can appropriate the economic benefits tend to ally with the sender state and reinforce its efforts to move the recipient's policy preference in the direction of the sender's intent. Third, incentives are unlikely to create an impetus to elude or undermine their influence through the search for third-party suppliers or create the economic conditions that invite new entrants. Finally, incentives convey more precise information to decision makers in the recipient state in a manner that is unlikely to be filtered or avoided by them.

Perhaps the best test of this book's contribution will be whether it generates additional theoretical investigations into the operation and effect of economic incentives. It does not pretend to be the last word on the subject, but hopes to be an interesting and useful start. One logical expansion of this work would be a "large N" study of incentives that seeks to strengthen, refine, or reject the hypotheses on the operation of economic incentives provided in chapter 2. For example, the relationship between the sender's market power and the success of attempted incentives might be operationalized without great difficulty.

Likewise, additional case studies or experimental designs could allow for closer empirical examination of other hypotheses. For example, the assertion that incentives communicate more clearly than other policy instruments because the recipient is less likely to screen the message could be explored using a different form of case study focusing more intensely on decision maker cognition and perception or could be approximated through an experimental approach. Another study might look at incentive cases with more variance on the dependent variable to explore the relationship between incentives and other factors that influence cooperative adjustment. Unlike this study, where the cases were a qualified success, by considering cases of more clear-cut success and failure one might better tease out relationships between incentives and other variables. The material for such studies is readily available. The use of an incentive strategy has arisen, for example, in recent U.S. relations with Iraq, Ukraine, Kazakhstan, North Korea, Vietnam, and others.[2] Moreover, because the United States is only one of many states that use or have used incentives, the number of meaningful incidents is substantial.

Although this book considers several questions related to the operation of economic incentives, many other important issues lie outside its scope. Regarding the dependent variable, the cases considered here do not attempt to reach far beyond the bilateral relationship. Like many studies of international relations, this one begins with the dyadic ties as the most basic form of interstate relations.[3] Although chapter 6 alludes to the third-party consequences of bilateral incentives, it does not explore this issue extensively. Many instances of attempted international cooperation involve multilateral relationships and settings, of course, and commend an application of some of the ideas developed here to that context. I anticipate that incentives operate better in multilateral, institutionalized settings, but this expectation should be examined empirically.

This study, by examining the potential of economic incentives, also commends further investigations of the power not only of incentives, but of other diffuse factors—norms, laws, public opinion, and others—shaping state preferences and behavior. Although not strictly defended in this book, the case studies suggest that noninstitutionalized cooperation may be more prevalent than previously acknowledged and that diffuse factors (like incentives) can affect interstate cooperation.

This book also claims to be of practical relevance to policymakers. Although the primary goal of chapter 2 and the case studies is to develop hypotheses in an area scholars have slighted, policymakers as well as academics can profit from a better understanding of incentives.

Ironically, perhaps, while incentives have been "undertheorized" in the international relations literature (despite considerable interest in economic coercion), they have not gone unnoticed by policymakers; indeed, their popularity as a policy instrument may be rising as defense budgets shrink. As noted, economic incentives are a widely available and often-used policy tool.

As policymakers consider the appropriateness of incentives to today's problems, they should understand, at a minimum, that economic sanctions and incentives operate in substantially different ways, serve divergent goals, and depend on distinctive factors for their success. Although both policies alter the payoffs facing states, they are not wholly interchangeable instruments. Incentives may be more appropriate instruments if the goal is long-run bilateral cooperation. If, however, the goal is deterrence, punishment, or displacement, then sanctions are likely to be the preferred policy instrument and incentives can be counterproductive or dangerous.

Further, for policymakers, the particular conditions needed for sanctions to work for compellant purposes are quite rigorous and rare: near monopoly power in the traded good; asymmetrical dependence of the target on the recipient; and swift and sure implementation. The necessary conditions for successful incentive policies are more widely available: the existence of, or potential for, a bilateral exchange relationship where the sender has in some way impeded full recognition of the trade gains available to the potential recipient (monopoly power is not necessary); a minimum degree of trust or confidence in the bilateral relationship; and steady, patient institutional application.

The time needed to lay the foundation and build a successful incentive strategy may be a luxury policymakers do not have in every instance. Still, hasty incentive strategies may be worse than no incentive strategy at all. Some institutional strength in the recipient state also is a prerequisite for successful incentives, because incentives require building a relationship and fulfilling promises by both parties.

Incentives are more likely to succeed, other things being equal, when certain conditions prevail in both the sender and recipient state. In the sender, supportive factors include market power in the relevant goods or technologies, strong and active societal actors, and receptive or pliant public opinion. In the recipient, helpful conditions include strong demand for the incentive goods or technologies, influential societal stakeholders who stand to benefit economically and otherwise from the incentive, and public opinion that attaches positive symbolic meaning to the incentive.

These insights may be a useful aid to policymakers, but they are not to substitute for policymakers' judgments. The decision to use an incentive strategy can only be made with actor-specific knowledge. The role of this book is to identify some of the relevant questions for a policymaker to consider in searching for and synthesizing that knowledge. Here, too, further studies should enhance the practical understanding of incentives.

Future policy-relevant research might differentiate between forms of economic incentives and their availability and operation. Some incentives, such as tariff reductions, may be of declining availability and importance as a tool of influence as average world tariffs have declined substantially over the past fifty years. On the other hand, nontariff barriers to trade such as "voluntary" export restraints have, by some measures, grown as a form of discrimination outside the GATT framework.[4] Figure 1 illustrates the recent growth of nontariff barriers to trade whose removal would represent an important potential incentive.[5] The possibility of relaxing nontariff barriers to trade and technology flows is a significant putative form of economic incentive that merits closer study. Likewise, technology transfer is an increasingly important feature in economic growth and development and is likely to continue to play an important role in international affairs. Capital transfers, which dwarf trade flows, are also subject to state manipulation and are another important policy instrument, although seldom studied as such.

In a powerful and influential work, Robert Axelrod and Robert Keohane remind us, "If governments are prepared to grope their way toward a

% of imports

Fig. 1. U.S. imports subject to "hard-core" nontariff barriers, 1981 and 1986

better coordinated future, scholars should be prepared to study the process."[6] Yet, perhaps because of their influence and that of others, scholars interested in international cooperation have focused intensively on institutionalized forms of cooperation, the role of regimes in cooperation, and strategies of specific reciprocity. This book implies that understanding patterns and processes of international cooperation could also benefit by widening the aperture of investigation beyond direct reciprocity and the role of institutions and regimes to look more closely at incentives and other, more diffuse, uninstitutional factors pertinent to the process of interstate cooperation.

Appendix

Wagner's point that political influence is exchanged for gains from trade can be broken down and illustrated through basic economic diagrams. The first illustration is an Edgeworth box representing a two country/two commodity trade-off. In figure 2, the sender country (S) and the recipient country (R) trade with each other for the economic goods G_1 and G_2. S_1 and R_1 are their no-gain-from-trade indifference curves, that is, certain trade agreements are equivalent to no trade at all for either country. Point C_* is their autarkic trading position. Between S_1 and R_1 both countries may benefit from trade under certain terms. Only on the contract curve ($C_1 C_2$), however, will both countries find no alternative terms of trade to improve one's satisfaction level from trade without hurting the other's— what economists call core Pareto-optimal allocations. A decision to open trade relations determines whether the two countries are within the area bounded by $S_1 R_1$. *Where* along the contract curve they trade will be determined by their respective factor endowments, which establish prices, in this case, C_{**}. Thus, a decision by S to lift political impediments preventing trade can improve the welfare of both S and R.

Another form of incentive occurs when S possesses a degree of market power in a traded good by virtue of technological supremacy and imperfect competition in the marketplace. The sender's attempt to exercise market power in shifting the terms of trade might take the form of an optimum tariff strategy or an export tax, in these instances. By exercising its market power, S would have moved the point of exchange off the contract curve to a point like C_{***} in figure 2—a point of lower utility for R. In this situation, S has the option of offering another variant of a trade incentive: by removing or lowering a tariff, for example, S can improve the terms of existing trade for the recipient (movement to point C_*) and increase R's welfare by enhancing R's gain from trade.

The welfare-enhancing effects of opening new trade as a form of incentive for R can be seen in figure 3. Figure 3 illustrates the gains to R as it moves from autarkic terms of trade (established by its consumer's pref-

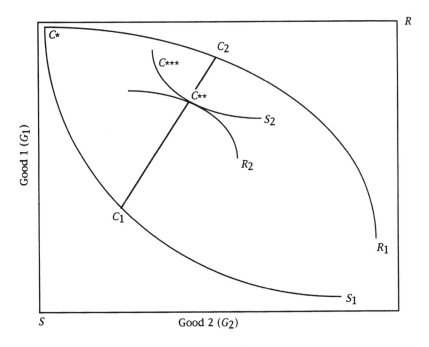

Fig. 2. Trade and market power

erences in conjunction with its production possibilities for Good 1 and Good 2). This autarkic situation is represented in figure 3 by point E at utility level U_0. Whenever there are autarkic price differences between S and R, there is a basis for profitable trade between them at some intermediate set of prices that lies between their respective domestic prices. The gain to S and R derives from the larger income they enjoy because of the higher price received for their exports and the lower price for their imports. In figure 3, if the price ratio in S were to involve a higher price of Good 2 (or a lower price of Good 1) and the two countries were to reopen trade by virtue of S lifting an embargo policy, a new price line, P_1, depicts the new level of production in R at point F_1 and the new level of consumption at point C_1. Country R would export uF_1 of Good 2 in exchange for uC_1 of imports of Good 1, thereby achieving a higher level of utility (the movement to U_1). The relaxation of a tariff or an export tax could be pictured in a similar fashion.

To use economic power for political concessions requires a second exchange. In the second exchange the sender uses new or unexploited advantage in the ongoing exchange of goods to purchase political concessions from country R in a second transaction. This second exchange can be

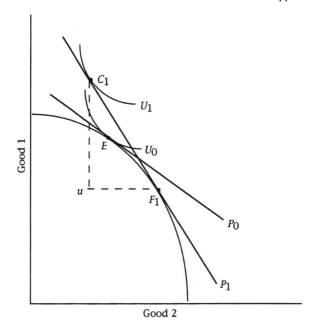

Fig. 3. Welfare improvement from economic incentive for recipient

illustrated by a similar Edgeworth box: figure 4. In this figure, newly created or exploitable gains from trade are arrayed along the vertical axis. This economic good can be exchanged for political concessions, which are arrayed along the horizontal axis of figure 4.

In this second exchange, S trades newly created or unexploited profits from trade for political concessions from R. $S_{1'}$ and $R_{1'}$ are countries S's and R's no-gain-from-economic-statecraft curves; that is, certain exchanges of economic gains for political concessions are equivalent to no exchange of the two values at all, which is point C_*. Both countries can use their bargaining power to reach a higher utility at point C_{**} on the new contract curve that exhausts all their bargaining power, as happened in the trade between economic goods. (Again, movement to higher levels of utility assumes S values the political concessions more than R does and that S is willing to swap gains from trade to get them).[1]

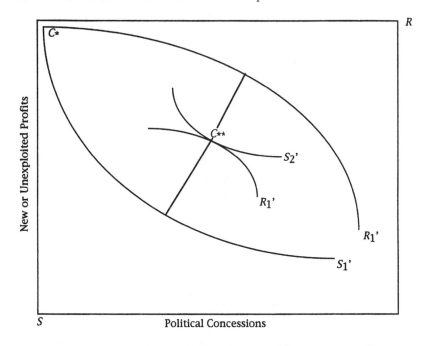

Fig. 4. Statecraft: Gains from trade exchanged for political concessions

Notes

Chapter 1

1. Like most studies of strategy, I am defining incentives and promises in terms of the sender's activities (an action undertaken by the sender to change the recipient's behavior), not in terms of the recipient's attitude (whether the recipient believes the sender's actions are an incentive or sanction). See David A. Baldwin, "Thinking About Threats," *Journal of Conflict Resolution* 15, no. 1 (March 1971): 72.

2. On the nature of coercive and noncoercive power see David A. Baldwin, "Power and Social Exchange," *American Political Science Review* 72, no. 4 (December 1978): 1229–32. In that article, Baldwin argues that all exchange relationships can be described in terms of conventional power concepts. Baldwin maintains, "To describe a power relationship in terms of A getting B to do something against his will is to obscure the heart of the power process, i.e., A's manipulation of the incentives (or opportunity costs) that B associates with various courses of action." See also, J. C. Harsanyi, "Measurement of Social Power, Opportunity Costs, and the Theory of Two-person Bargaining Games," *Behavioral Science* (January 1962): 67–80. For other broad conceptualization of power see John Gaventa, *Power and Powerlessness* (Urbana: University of Illinois Press, 1980); Steven Lukes, *Power: A Radical View* (London: MacMillan, 1974).

3. For a review of some of this literature see Russell J. Leng and Hugh G. Wheeler, "Influence Strategies, Success, and War," *Journal of Conflict Resolution* 23, no. 4 (December 1979): 655–84; Joshua S. Goldstein and John R. Freeman, *Three-Way Street: Strategic Reciprocity in World Politics* (Chicago: University of Chicago Press, 1991), chap. 1.

4. David Baldwin, *Economic Statecraft* (Princeton, NJ: Princeton University Press, 1985), pp. 40–50.

5. Ibid.

6. See George Liska, *The New Statecraft: Foreign Aid in American Foreign Policy* (Chicago: University of Chicago Press, 1960); David Baldwin, *Economic Development and American Foreign Policy* (Chicago: University of Chicago Press, 1966); Joan M. Nelson, *Aid, Influence and Foreign Policy* (New York: Macmillan, 1968);

Robert F. Zimmerman, *Dollars, Diplomacy, and Dependency: Dilemmas of U.S. Economic Aid* (Boulder, CO: Lynne Rienner, 1993).

7. David Obey and Carol Lancaster, "Funding Foreign Aid," *Foreign Policy*, no. 71 (summer 1988): 149. In support of the instrumental use of foreign aid see Lynne Dratler Finney, "Development Assistance—A Tool of Foreign Policy," *Case Western Reserve Journal of International Law* 15 (spring 1983): 213–52.

8. See David Baldwin, *Economic Statecraft*, p. 11, n. 15. But see Louis Kriesberg, "Carrots, Sticks, De-escalation: U.S.-Soviet and Arab-Israeli Relations," *Armed Forces and Society* 13, no. 3 (spring 1987): 403–23; Fred Lawson, "Using Positive Sanctions to End International Conflicts: Iran and Arab Gulf Countries," *Journal of Peace Research* 20, no. 4 (1983): 311–28.

9. See David Baldwin, *Economic Statecraft;* M. S. Daoudi and M. S. Dajani, *Economic Sanctions: Ideals and Experience* (London: Routledge & Kegan Paul, 1983); Gary Hufbauer, Jeffrey Schott, and Kimberly Ann Elliott, *Economic Sanctions Reconsidered* (Washington, DC: Institute for International Economics, 1985); Stephanie Ann Lenway, "Economic Sanctions and Statecraft," *International Organization* 42, no. 2 (spring 1988): 397–426. Scholarly interest and insights into economic sanctions have undergone several phases. After World War I, sanctions were viewed as a viable, effective means of resolving international differences short of the use of military force. By the late 1960s, however, economic sanctions were in disrepute as costly and ineffective. Current literature questions the assumptions that economic coercion does not work. Recent studies suggest that while a sanction may not bring a change in the behavior of the target state, it may bring some influence to bear and serve a variety of other goals without incurring the costs associated with military intervention. This judgment, combined with the demands of political expediency or the lack of policy alternatives, may explain the repeated resort to economic sanctions.

10. On this conceptual bias see David Baldwin, *Economic Statecraft*, pp. 117–18.

11. See Klaus Knorr, *The Power of Nations* (New York: Basic Books, 1975).

12. David Baldwin, *Economic Statecraft*, p. 46.

13. William Long, *U.S. Export Control Policy: Executive Autonomy Versus Congressional Reform* (New York: Columbia University Press, 1989).

14. David Baldwin, "The Power of Positive Sanctions," *World Politics* 24, no. 1 (October 1971): 24. Although incentives and sanctions create the possibility for the other and can be viewed as an incentive by the sender and a veiled threat by the recipient, these intertemporal and intersubjective shifts should not confuse the reader into believing that sanctions and incentives are indistinguishable instruments, nor does it imply that they operate identically.

15. Wendt also concedes, "The 'problem' with all this is that we lack a self-evident way to conceptualize these entities and their relationship." Alexander Wendt, "The Agent-Structure Problem in International Relations Theory," *International Organization* 41, no. 3 (summer 1987): 338.

16. David Dessler, "What's at Stake in the Agent-Structure Debate," *International Organization* 43, no. 3 (summer 1989): 456.

17. Alexander Wendt, "The Agent-Structure Problem," p. 362.

18. Ibid.

19. Robert Keohane, *After Hegemony* (Princeton, NJ: Princeton University Press, 1984), p. 80.

20. Ibid., p. 51.

21. Ibid., pp. 51–52.

22. Ibid.

23. Ibid. While this bright line distinction between cooperation and harmony drawn by Robert Keohane is useful for this study, others view cooperation as having more subtle gradations. See Benjamin Miller, "Explaining Great Power Cooperation in Conflict Management," *World Politics* 45, no. 1 (October 1992): 12.

24. Terry Moe, "Interests, Institutions, and Positive Theory: The Politics of the NLRB," in *Studies in American Political Development, vol. 2,* ed. Karen Orren and Stephen Skowronek (New Haven, CT: Yale University Press, 1987), p. 283.

25. Andrew Moravcsik, "Preferences and Power in the European Community: A Liberal Intergovernmentalist Approach," *Journal of Common Market Studies* 31 (October 1993): 478. Jeffrey Legro makes a similar point, "International cooperation can be conceptualized as part of a two-step process. One part involves the formation of preferences of actors, the second interaction among the preferences of actors that leads to an outcome. An understanding of both is necessary to explain behavior." Jeffrey W. Legro, "Preferences and International Cooperation," paper prepared for the annual meeting of the American Political Science Association, Washington, DC, September 2–5, 1993, p. 3.

26. See Joseph Grieco, *Cooperation Among Nations* (Ithaca, NY: Cornell University Press, 1990), chap. 1; Arthur Stein, *Why Nations Cooperate* (Ithaca, NY: Cornell University Press, 1990). See generally, Hans J. Morganthau, *Politics Among Nations,* 5th ed. (New York: Alfred A. Knopf, 1978). Compare with Duncan Snidal, "International Cooperation Among Relative Gain Maximizers," *International Studies Quarterly* 35, no. 4 (December 1991): 387–402.

27. Robert Jervis, "Cooperation Under the Security Dilemma," *World Politics* 30, no. 2 (January 1978): 177; Joseph S. Nye, Jr., "Nuclear Learning and U.S.-Soviet Security Regimes," *International Organization* 41, no. 3 (summer 1987): 372.

28. See, for example, Jervis, "Cooperation Under the Security Dilemma," p. 177. In critiquing realism, Nye has noted, "Hopes that a system of international law and organization could provide collective security, which would replace the need for self-help inherent in the security dilemma, were disappointed in 1939" Nye, "Nuclear Learning," p. 372.

29. Inis Claude, Jr., *Power and International Relations* (New York: Random House, 1962). In contrast, David Baldwin's definition of coercion includes anything that adds or subtracts from the target's cost-benefit analysis and, therefore, explicitly includes promised or actual rewards as well as threats and punishments (*Economic Statecraft,* pp. 38–39).

30. See Kenneth Waltz, *Theory of International Politics* (Reading, MA: Addison-Wesley, 1979), pp. 117–28.

31. Because this work concerns commercial exchange and cooperation, it raises, for many, liberal notions that peace is the natural effect of trade. It is important, however, to distinguish this study from liberal economic theories of peace. First, this study does not presume that there is natural harmony of interests between

states that more open commercial exchange will facilitate and maintain. Rather, I assume that conflict, cooperation, and harmony are all present in varying degrees and are natural conditions in international relations. Indeed, the focus on cooperation implies the definite possibility of conflict, rather than harmony, as the likely state of affairs. Instead, I am arguing that trade and technology transfer can be used to promote interstate *cooperation,* that is, other-regarding policy adjustment. The goal of this study is to propose the conditions under which incentives will and will not induce cooperation. I also do not equate cooperation with peace or imply that cooperation is necessarily good for the international system. Conceivably, states could cooperate through the use of incentives for ends that might be destabilizing or destructive when viewed from a third-party or systemic perspective.

32. Stein, *Why Nations Cooperate,* pp. 7–10; Grieco, *Cooperation Among Nations,* pp. 4–9, 28. See John Conybeare, *Trade Wars* (New York: Columbia University Press, 1987); Keohane, *After Hegemony.*

33. Keohane, *After Hegemony,* p. 57.

34. See Nye, "Nuclear Learning," pp. 371–402.

35. Robert Axelrod, *The Evolution of Cooperation* (New York: Basic Books, 1984).

36. Keohane, *After Hegemony.*

37. International interactions can be modeled using a wide variety of other games as well. The literature is extensive. See, for example, Glenn H. Synder and Paul Diesing, *Conflict Among Nations: Bargaining, Decision Making, and System Structure in International Crises* (Princeton, NJ: Princeton University Press, 1977); Stein, *Why Nations Cooperate.* For a critique of Prisoner's Dilemma and other models as representative of international relations, see R. Harrison Wagner, "The Theory of Games and the Problem of International Cooperation," *American Political Science Review* 77, no. 2 (June 1983): 330–46.

38. Robert Jervis, "Realism, Game Theory, and Cooperation," *World Politics* 40, no. 3 (April 1988): 318.

39. Ibid.

40. See Joseph Grieco, "Anarchy and the Limits of Cooperation: A Realist Critique of the Newest Liberal Institutionalism," *International Organization* 42, no. 3 (summer 1988): 493.

41. Robert Axelrod and Robert Keohane, "Achieving Cooperation Under Anarchy: Strategies and Institutions," *World Politics* 38, no. 1 (October 1985): 227–32.

42. Jervis, "Realism, Game Theory, and Cooperation," p. 319. See also Deborah Welch Larson, "The Psychology of Reciprocity in International Relations," *Negotiation Journal* 4, no. 3 (July 1988): 281–83.

43. Jervis, "Realism, Game Theory, and Cooperation," p. 322. Benjamin Cohen likewise notes the limiting effects of leaving a state's payoff environment and preferences outside the theoretic model:

> The limitations, as every serious game theorist knows, lie in the methodology of game theory itself. . . . Even more critical is the familiar problem of specifying player motivations. Game models . . . provide insights into the strategic

choices that can be expected of individual players once the orderings of all the actors' preferences are fully detailed . . . [N]othing in the essential logic of game theory tells us how the configurations of preferences get to be determined in the first place. By their very nature, game models are silent on the subject of what initially motivates players. Preference orderings at the outset are simply assumed to be exogenously—that is, arbitrarily—determined . . . The limitation of even the most ambitious applications of game theory lies in the tendency to concentrate on what comes out of state conceptions of self-interest rather than what goes into them.

Benjamin Cohen, "The Political Economy of International Trade," *International Organization* 44, no. 2 (spring 1990): 276–78.

44. In psychology, changing the responses of actors by rearranging the rewards and punishments that follow certain behavior is known as "operant conditioning"—teaching a subject to operate in its world in ways that produce certain desired consequences. The main principle of operant conditioning states that "the frequency of any spontaneously occurring response may be increased or decreased if it is followed by an appropriate stimulus. . . . The stimulus has either rewarding or punishing properties . . ." To maximize operant conditioning, according to B. F. Skinner and others, the reinforcing reward or punishment must be delivered immediately after the response occurs. Delays in reinforcement slow down the rate of desired adaptation in behavior. Consistent with this notion, international relations theory focuses on immediately reciprocated reinforcers (carrots and sticks) and ignores the possibility that more delayed, protracted, and diffuse incentives can also condition behavior. This book does not assume that the behavior of states is necessarily conditioned in the same way as individual subjects. See Harry I. Kalish, *From Behavioral Science to Behavior Modification* (New York: McGraw-Hill, 1981), p. 122; John M. Darley, Sam Glucksberg, and Ronald A. Kinchla, *Psychology,* 4th ed. (Englewood Cliffs, NJ: Prentice Hall, 1984).

45. For a recent iteration of this debate, see Joseph Grieco, Robert Powell, and Duncan Snidal, "The Relative Gains Problem for International Cooperation," *American Political Science Review* 87, no. 3 (September 1993): 729–43.

46. Joseph Nye, Jr., "Neo-realism and Neo-liberalism," *World Politics* 40, no. 2 (January 1988): 238–39.

47. Stein, *Why Nations Cooperate,* p. 10.

48. Ibid.

49. The problem of improving our understanding of the forces that shape state preferences echoes through the literature. For example, Charles Lipson maintains that theory must "Consider the subtle ways that environmental conditions shape international interactions in particular issues [and] the patterned incentives and disincentives for national choice . . ." Charles Lipson, "International Cooperation in Economic and Security Affairs," *World Politics* 37, no. 1 (1984): 22.

50. Helen Milner, "International Theories of Cooperation Among Nations: Strengths and Weaknesses," *World Politics* 44, no. 3 (April 1992): 317–47.

51. Ibid., p. 489.

52. See Robert Gilpin, *U.S. Power and the Multinational Corporation* (New

York: Basic Books, 1975); Stephen Krasner, "State Power and the Structure of International Trade," *World Politics* 28, no. 3 (April 1976): 317–47; Peter Katzenstein, Introduction and Conclusion to "Between Power and Plenty: Foreign Economic Policies of Advanced Industrial States," *International Organization* 31, no. 4 (autumn 1977): 587–606, 879–920.

53. Peter F. Cowhey, "'States' and 'Politics' in American Foreign Policy," in *International Trade Policies,* ed. John S. Odell and Thomas D. Willet (Ann Arbor: University of Michigan Press, 1993), p. 225.

54. One of the conceptual shortcomings of statist theory has been a lack of clarity and consistency in defining "the state." See Stephen D. Krasner, "Approaches to the State: Alternative Conceptualizations and Historical Dynamics," *Comparative Politics* 16, no. 2 (January 1984): 223–46.

55. See John Ikenberry, "Conclusion: An Institutional Approach to American Foreign Policy," *International Organization* 42, no. 1 (winter 1988): 219–43; David A. Lake, "The State in American Trade Strategy in the Pre-Hegemonic Era," *International Organization* 42, no. 1 (winter 1988): 33–58; William J. Long, *U.S. Export Control Policy: Executive Autonomy Versus Congressional Reform.*

56. Peter Gourevitch, "The Second Image Reversed: The International Sources of Domestic Policies," *International Organization* 32, no. 4 (autumn 1978): 903.

57. Krasner, "Approaches to the State," p. 225.

58. Stephen D. Krasner, "Sovereignty: An Institutional Perspective," *Comparative Political Studies* 21, no. 1 (April 1988): 71–72.

59. Robert Keohane, "International Institutions: Two Approaches," *International Studies Quarterly* 32, no. 4 (December 1988): 386.

60. See, for example, Robert A. Dahl, *Pluralist Democracy in the United States: Conflict and Consent* (Chicago: Rand McNally, 1967); Nelson W. Polsby, *Congress and the Presidency* (Englewood Cliffs, NJ: Prentice-Hall, 1973); David Truman, *The Governmental Process: Political Interests and Public Opinion* (New York: Knopf, 1971). With regard to relative state strength, see Stephen D. Krasner, *Defending the National Interest* (Princeton, NJ: Princeton University Press, 1978).

61. See Krasner, "Approaches to the State," pp. 227–29.

62. See Graham T. Allison, *Essence of Decision: Explaining the Cuban Missile Crisis* (Boston, MA: Little, Brown and Company, 1971); Morton H. Halperin, *Bureaucratic Politics and Foreign Policy* (Washington, DC: Brookings Institution, 1974).

63. See, for example, Herbert A. Simon, *Administrative Behavior* (New York: Free Press, 1946); Allison, *Essence of Decision.* On individual decision making see, for example, John Steinbrunner, *The Cybernetic Theory of Decision: New Dimensions of Political Analysis* (Princeton, NJ: Princeton University Press, 1974); Michael Brecher, *Decisions in Israel's Foreign Policy* (New Haven, CT: Yale University Press, 1974); Richard Ned Lebow, *Between Peace and War* (Baltimore, MD: Johns Hopkins University Press, 1981); Donald R. Kinder and Janet A. Weiss, "In Lieu of Rationality: Psychological Perspectives on Foreign Policy Decision Making," *Journal of Conflict Resolution* 22, no. 4 (December 1978): 707–35.

64. Robert Jervis, "Hypotheses on Misperception," *World Politics* 20, no. 3

(April 1968): 454–79; *Perception and Misperception in International Politics* (Princeton, NJ: Princeton University Press, 1976).

65. Jervis, *Perception and Misperception*, pp. 187–202.

66. See for example, Irving L. Janis and Leon Mann, *Decision-making: A Psychological Analysis of Conflict, Choice, and Commitment* (New York: Free Press, 1977).

67. Keohane, *After Hegemony*, p. 56.

68. See Alexander L. George, "Case Studies and Theory Development," paper presented to the second annual Symposium on Information Processing in Organizations, Carnegie Mellon University, October 15–16, 1982; Alexander L. George and Timothy J. McKeown, "Case Studies and Theories in Organizational Decision-making," in R. Coulum and R. Smith, eds., *Advances in Information Processing in Organizations* (Greenwich, CT: JAI Press, 1985), pp. 21–58.

69. In making this point by example, Deborah Larson asks, "Was Gorbachev's offer at the Reykjavik summit to eliminate nuclear weapons in ten years a cooperative move or a defection? It depends on whether one believes that the Soviet leader was carried away by the exhilaration of the moment or was trying to trap an aged, ill-informed President and divide NATO." "Psychology of Reciprocity," p. 286.

70. See Arend Lijphart, "Comparative Politics and the Comparative Method," *American Political Science Review* 65, no. 3 (September 1971): 685–86.

71. Milner, "International Theories," p. 468.

72. Baldwin, *Economic Statecraft*, p. 22.

73. Ibid.

74. Alexander L. George, David K. Hall, and William E. Simons, *The Limits of Coercive Diplomacy* (Boston, MA: Little, Brown and Co., 1971).

75. Baldwin, *Economic Statecraft*, p. 9.

76. Larson, "Psychology of Reciprocity," p. 297.

Chapter 2

1. Arthur Stein's study of cooperation notes that structural features, such as the nature of technology and the nature of knowledge, can transform state interests and the prospects for international cooperation (*Why Nations Cooperate*, p. 49).

2. Albert O. Hirschman, *National Power and the Structure of Foreign Trade* (Berkeley, CA: University of California Press, 1980), p. 12.

3. Ibid., chap. 1.

4. R. Harrison Wagner, "Economic Interdependence, Bargaining Power, and Political Influence," *International Organization* 42, no. 3 (summer 1988): 462–72.

5. Because the welfare of both parties is enhanced, this form of power is considered noncoercive by Wagner and others.

6. Wagner, "Economic Interdependence," p. 473.

7. Ibid., pp. 473–79.

8. For example, the simple and widely used Cobb-Douglas production function establishes the relationship showing the maximum amount of output capable of being produced by every set of capital and labor inputs, *for a given state of technical knowledge.* The formula is:

$$Q = A \, L^{\alpha} \, K^{\beta}$$

where
   Q = output in physical units
   L = quantity of labor input
   K = quantity of capital input

A, α (alpha), and β (beta) are positive parameters. A refers to the level of technology, alpha is the output elasticity of labor, and beta the output elasticity of capital.

9. See U.S. Department of Labor, "Productivity and the Economy," *Bulletin of the Bureau of Labor Statistics,* no. 1926 (Washington, DC: U.S. Government Printing Office, 1977), p. 63.

10. Robert M. Solow, "Technological Change and the Aggregate Production Function," *Review of Economics and Statistics* 39 (1957): 312–20.

11. Only the science and technology branch of international relations writings recognizes the potential of technology transfer as a tool of statecraft, but it has not examined its effects. Despite noting the foreign policy potential of technology and speculating on its effectiveness, this literature has not generated hypotheses or in-depth studies of the role of technology as an instrument of national influence. In those rare instances when it addresses the relationship of technology to international cooperation, it confines itself to examining international cooperation *in science and technology,* rather than the use of scientific or technological transfer as an independent factor as it affects cooperation across a broader range of state interests. See Brigitte Schroeder Gudehus, "Science, Technology Policy and Foreign Policy," in *Science, Technology and Society,* ed. Ina Spiegal-Rosing and Derek de Solla Price (Beverly Hills, CA: Sage Publications, 1977), p. 479; Mitchel B. Wallerstein, ed., *Scientific and Technological Cooperation among Advanced Industrialized Countries: The Role of the United States* (Washington, DC: National Academy Press, 1984), p. 19.

12. The real cost to the capital donor of foreign aid is the income forgone as a result of the outflow of capital, given alternative possible uses for the same funds.

13. Jervis, "Realism, Game Theory, and Cooperation," p. 322.

14. See generally, Milner, "International Theories," pp. 466–97; Peter Gourevitch, "The Second Image Reversed: The International Sources of Domestic Policies," *International Organization* 32 (autumn 1978): 881–912.

15. As noted, this trade-off may not be necessary if the sender is moving away from embargo and creating new trade through an incentive policy.

16. On the merits of this two-level approach see Robert Putnam, "Diplomacy and Domestic Politics: The Logic of Two-Level Games," *International Organization* 42, no. 3 (summer 1988): 427–60. See also Jeffrey W. Knopf, "Beyond Two-Level Games: Domestic-International Interaction in the INF Episode," paper prepared for the annual meeting of the American Political Science Association, Washington, DC, September 2–5, 1993.

17. In perhaps the most comprehensive treatment of this issue, Robert G. Sutter concludes: "The American business community generally has not exerted a major influence on the course of recent U.S.-China policy and did not push strongly for

rapid forward movement in normalization of relations with the PRC, which presumably would have led to improved U.S. economic opportunities in the PRC." Robert G. Sutter, *The China Quandary: Domestic Determinants of U.S. China Policy 1972–1982* (Boulder, CO: Westview Press, 1983), p. 128.

18. Otto Wolff von Amerongen, "Economic Sanctions as a Foreign Policy Tool?" *International Security* 5 (fall 1980): 160.

19. Hufbauer, Schott, and Elliott, *Economic Sanctions Reconsidered,* pp. 11, 86.

20. Ibid., p. 86.

21. On the growth in enthusiasm for China trade among U.S. businesses, see Sutter, *China Quandary,* chap. 7.

22. Hufbauer, Schott, and Elliott, *Economic Sanctions Reconsidered,* p. 10; Peter Wallenstein, "Characteristics of Economic Sanctions," *Journal of Peace Research* 5, no. 3 (summer 1968): 248–67; Margaret Doxey, "International Sanctions: A Framework for Analysis with Special Reference to the U.N. and South Africa," *International Organization* 26, no. 3 (summer 1972): 527–50; Jerrold Green, "Strategies for Evading Economic Sanctions," in *Dilemmas of Economic Coercion: Sanctions in World Politics,* ed. M. Nincic and P. Wallensteen (New York: Praeger, 1983).

23. See, for example, Patrick Clawson, *How Has Saddam Hussein Survived?* (Washington, DC: National Defense University, 1993); Anna P. Schreiber, "Economic Coercion as an Instrument of Policy: U.S. Measures Against Cuba and the Dominican Republic," *World Politics* 25, no. 3 (April 1973): 387–413.

24. David M. Rowe, "The Domestic Political Economy of International Economic Sanctions," paper prepared for the annual meeting of the American Political Science Association, Washington, DC, September 2–5, 1993, pp. 8–11.

25. Ibid.

26. Ibid.

27. See Mitchell Reiss, *Without the Bomb: The Politics of Nuclear Nonproliferation* (New York: Columbia University Press, 1988); Wilhelm Agrell, "The Bomb that Never Was: The Rise and Fall of the Swedish Nuclear Weapons Program," in *Arms Races: Technological Political Dynamics,* ed. Nils Peter Gleditsch and Olan Njolstud (Oslo, Norway: International Peace Research Institute, 1990).

28. Lisa L. Martin, *Coercive Cooperation: Explaining Multilateral Economic Sanctions* (Princeton, NJ: Princeton University Press, 1992), p. 3.

29. This loss-aversion tendency helps explain why states are more concerned about preventing a decline in their reputation or credibility than about increasing it by a comparable amount, or why they are more concerned about "falling dominoes" than hopeful that states would bandwagon in their favor. Jack S. Levy, "Prospect Theory and International Relations: Theoretical Applications and Analytical Problems," *Political Psychology* 13, no. 2 (June 1992): 284–85.

30. Janis and Mann, *Decision-making.*

31. Although misperception does not always lead to noncooperative outcomes, it does when an actor's choice is contingent on the actions of others and the misunderstood actor has a dominant strategy of noncooperation or is a tit-for-tat reciprocator. Arthur Stein, "When Misperception Matters," *World Politics* 34, no. 4 (July 1982): 505–26.

32. See Grieco, *Cooperation Among Nations,* n. 26.

33. The sanctions literature concludes that sanctions may communicate, on the one hand, the sender's strength and resolve or, on the other hand, the sender's weakness. Compare James Barber, "Economic Sanctions as a Policy Instrument," *International Affairs* 55, no. 3 (July 1979): 367–84, and James Mayall, "The Sanctions Problem in International Economic Relations," *International Affairs* 60, no. 4 (October 1984): 631–42, with Fredrik Hoffman, "The Functions of Economic Sanctions: A Comparative Analysis," *Journal of Peace Research* 4, no. 2 (spring 1967): 140–59.

34. John R. Raser, "Learning and Affect in International Politics," *Journal of Peace Research* 2, no. 3 (summer 1965): 223.

35. On the possible value of ambiguity in threats and promises see David Baldwin, "Thinking About Threats," p. 75.

36. Wendt, "The Agent-Structure Problem."

Chapter 3

1. Although policymakers rarely challenged the notion that proliferation was disadvantageous, academics have toyed with the idea that the spread of nuclear weapons could produce the same stabilizing and deterrent effects between other countries as that allegedly achieved by the United States and the Soviet Union. See, for example, Kenneth Waltz, *The Spread of Nuclear Weapons: More May be Better,* Adelphi Paper no. 171 (London: International Institute for Strategic Studies, 1981).

2. Quoted in Mason Willrich, *Non-Proliferation Treaty: Framework for Nuclear Arms Control* (Charlottesville, VA: Michie Company, 1969), p. 1.

3. See, for example, Lawrence Scheinman, "The Pendulum Swings While the Clock Ticks," in *The Nonproliferation Predicament,* ed. Joseph F. Pilat (New Brunswick: Transaction Books, 1985), p. 15.

4. Eisenhower's speech does not use the term *safeguards.* Instead he referred to a new international agency with responsibility to protect the bank of fissionable material. The concept of safeguards was later incorporated into the statute of the International Atomic Energy Agency after it had been used in the U.S. Atomic Energy Act of 1954. Sigmund Eklund, "Reliable Supply: Respecting the 'Rules of the Game,'" in *Atoms for Peace: An Analysis After Thirty Years,* ed. Joseph F. Pilat, Robert E. Pendley, and Charles K. Ebinger (Boulder, CO: Westview Press, 1983), p. 163.

5. U.S. Congress. House. Committee on Science and Technology. Subcommittee on Energy Research and Production. Historical and Political Framework of Safeguards. Report prepared by Gerald F. Tape. 98th Cong., 2d sess., 1983.

6. James R. Schlesinger, "Atoms for Peace Revisited," in Pilat, Pendley, and Ebinger, *Atoms for Peace,* p. 9.

7. Gerald F. Tape, "The Fabric of Cooperation," in Pilat, Pendley, and Ebinger, *Atoms for Peace,* p. 60. In fact, by 1953 at least ten nations were actively pursuing nuclear technology, and the Soviet Union was cooperating with China in nuclear matters.

8. H. L. Nieburg, *Nuclear Secrecy and Foreign Policy* (Washington, DC: Public Affairs Press, 1964), p. 79.

9. Philip Mullenbach, *Civilian Nuclear Power: Economic Issues and Policy Formulation* (New York: Twentieth Century Fund, 1963), p. 264.

10. Dwight D. Eisenhower, *Public Papers of the Presidents of the United States* (Washington, DC: Government Printing Office, 1957), pp. 813–22.

11. Steven J. Baker, *Commercial Nuclear Power and Nuclear Proliferation,* Peace Studies Occasional Paper no. 5, Cornell University, May 1975, p. 3.

12. The AEA became the legislative foundation for American domestic and international efforts in atomic energy. The AEA declared that "until effective and enforceable international safeguards against the use of atomic energy for destructive purposes have been established, there shall be no exchange with other nations with respect to the use of atomic energy for industrial purposes." Specifically, the AEA prohibited the export of goods, including fissionable materials (uranium, plutonium, and thorium), services, or information related to atomic energy. The legislation permitted the export under license of certain component parts of reactor facilities and the source material of radioactive isotopes for research purposes. However, the AEA made clear that American scientists and American industry were explicitly prohibited from engaging "directly or indirectly—in the production of any fissionable material outside the United States." Because of proliferation concerns, the AEA maintained an absolute government monopoly of all fissionable material or facilities that could produce such material. The legislation prohibited the export or dissemination of "restricted data," defined then to include all data "concerning the manufacture or utilization of atomic weapons, the production of fissionable materials, or the use of fissionable materials in the production of power." This broad definition encompassed almost all the existing knowledge of atomic energy. The AEA further prescribed penalties for violations, including the death penalty for those who disclosed atomic secrets to foreign governments. The AEA essentially prohibited virtually all international collaboration in atomic energy for nearly a decade. Likewise, prohibitions and stringent licensing provisions made meaningful private sector participation in the nuclear power field impossible. Atomic Energy Act of 1946. Pub.L. 585.

13. Nieburg, *Nuclear Secrecy and Foreign Policy,* p. 42.

14. U.S. Atomic Energy Commission, 1954, *International Cooperation in the Peaceful Uses of Atomic Energy Through the Instrument of the Bilateral Agreement for Cooperation,* republished in U.S. Congress, Joint Committee on Atomic Energy, *Background Information for the Review of the International Atomic Policies and Programs of the United States,* vol. 2, 80th Cong., 2d. sess., October 1960, p. 424 [hereafter cited as Joint Committee Report].

15. United States Code Annotated, vol. 42, section 2014 (1954).

16. William C. Potter, *Nuclear Power and Nonproliferation* (Cambridge, MA: Oelgeschlager, Gunn, and Hain, 1982), p. 39.

17. See U.S. National Security Council, Document 5507/2, "Statement of Policy on Peaceful Uses of Atomic Energy, General Considerations," March 12, 1955, p. 12.

18. U.S. Department of State, Treaties and Other International Acts Series (T.I.A.S.), no. 3775.

19. U.S. Department of State, Memorandum of Howard A. Robinson for Gerald C. Smith, "European Perspectives on Recent American Moves in the Field of Atomic Energy," October, 21, 1954.

20. Mullenbach, *Civilian Nuclear Power,* p. 286.

21. By 1962, an AEC report on civilian nuclear power emphatically concluded that nuclear power "is on the threshold of economic competitiveness. . . . [R]elatively modest assistance by the AEC will assure the crossing of that threshold and bring about widespread acceptance by the utility industry." Steven L. DelSesto, *Science, Politics and Controversy: Civilian Power in the United States 1946–1974* (Boulder, CO: Westview Press, 1987), p. 81.

22. Duncan Burn, *The Political Economy of Nuclear Energy* (London: Institute of Economic Affairs, 1967), p. 11.

23. William Walker and Måns Lonnroth, *Nuclear Power Struggles* (London: Allen & Unwin, 1983), p. 25; George Quester, *The Politics of Nuclear Proliferation* (Baltimore: Johns Hopkins University Press, 1973), p. 19.

24. These benefits included: access to AEC libraries, site visits, and training; unclassified reports and information on reactor development, chemical reprocessing, and fuel fabrication; Export-Import Bank loans to finance the costs of reactor construction and deferred payment plans for nuclear materials; financial assistance of up to $350,000 to defray the cost of building a nuclear research reactor (granted in 1958); and financial grants for equipment. Amendments to the U.S.-Swedish research reactor agreement liberalized the provisions to make highly enriched fuel available to material testing reactors. See Joint Committee Report, pp. 130–31, 163, 185, 271, 279, 358–59.

25. This agreement superseded the research reactor agreements, permitted the export of a larger quantity of nuclear materials consistent with the needs of nuclear power generation, and provided for stricter safeguards on its peaceful use. U.S. Department of State, Treaties and Other International Acts Series, no. 6076.

26. Interview data, Stockholm, September 9, 1992.

27. Ibid.

28. Thomas B. Johansson, "Sweden's Abortive Nuclear Weapons Project," *Bulletin of the Atomic Scientists* 42, no. 3 (March 1986): 33. See also Reiss, *Without the Bomb,* p. 39.

29. Agrell, "The Bomb That Never Was," p. 156.

30. Lars Wallin, "Sweden," in *Security with Nuclear Weapons: Different Perspectives on National Security,* ed. Regina Cowen Karp (Stockholm: Stockholm International Peace Research Institute and Oxford University Press, 1991), p. 361.

31. Agrell, "The Bomb That Never Was," p. 157.

32. Wallin, "Sweden," p. 362.

33. Paul A. Cole, *Neutralité du jour,* Ph.D. diss., Johns Hopkins University, 1990, p. 383. See also Martin Fehrm, "Sweden," in *Nuclear Non-proliferation: The Why and the Wherefore,* ed. Jozef Goldblat (London: Taylor & Francis, 1985), p. 213.

34. Johansson, "Sweden's Abortive Nuclear Weapons Project," pp. 31–34;

Christer Larsson, "History of the Swedish Atomic Bomb, 1945–1972," *Ny Teknik* (April 1985).

35. Jerome H. Garris, *Sweden and the Spread of Nuclear Weapons: A Study in Restraint,* Ph.D. diss., University of California at Los Angeles, 1972, p. 43; Jan Prawitz, "Sweden—A Non-Nuclear Weapon State," in *Security, Order, and the Bomb,* ed. Johan Jorgen Holst (Oslo: Universitetsforlaget, 1972), p. 62.

36. In 1949, AB Atomenergi launched plans for the development of such reactors, a program known as the "Blue-Yellow line" (for the colors of the Swedish flag) or "Swedish line." Initially, the natural uranium approach held several advantages for Sweden. Swedish resource infrastructure appeared capable of developing reactor fuel from large domestic deposits of low-grade uranium ore. Swedish officials also believed they could manufacture or obtain sufficient heavy water supplies. The heavy water approach also was the prevailing technology in the nuclear programs of France, Canada, and the United Kingdom, providing models for the Swedish program. In contrast, the technology to enrich uranium for LWRs was available only from the United States or would have required a huge expenditure of money and expertise to develop uranium enrichment facilities. Accepting enriched uranium from the United States would carry unwanted restrictions on its use. James Jasper, *Nuclear Politics: Energy and the State in the United States, Sweden, and France* (Princeton, NJ: Princeton University Press, 1990), p. 65.

37. Fehrm, "Sweden," pp. 213–14.

38. Interview data, Stockholm, September 10, 1992.

39. Christer Larsson argues that the basis for FOA's plans was a reactor program that would be maximized primarily for the production of weapons-grade plutonium and secondarily for the production of heat and electricity. This intent, he suggests, determined the selection of reactor technology as well: natural uranium and heavy water, which provided the most effective conversion process to plutonium (Pu-239). Larsson, "Swedish Atom Bomb." See also Reiss, *Without the Bomb,* pp. 43–44.

40. Agrell, "The Bomb That Never Was," p. 159.

41. Interview data, Stockholm, September 13, 1992. A Ministry of Defense study in response to such allegations asserted:

> The military authorities' possibility of directing the civil nuclear energy program to their aims was, however, not at all so great as has been asserted. . . . In my judgment, the choice in 1956 of reactors for the civil nuclear-energy program was, first of all, made for energy policy reasons, even if the military aspects appear to have been an important by-motive. And it is my opinion an indisputable fact that the Parliament was informed of the connection between the civil and military aspects.

Olof Forssberg, Chief Legal Advisor, Ministry of Defense, Svensk Karnvapan-Forskning [Swedish Nuclear Weapons Research] 1945–1972, April 21, 1987, pp. 7–8.

42. In a speech in December 1952, Air Force Chief of Staff General Bengt Nordenskiold urged equipping Sweden's armed forces with nuclear weapons.

Specifically, he claimed that small aircraft could carry low-yield, tactical atomic bombs and use them against seaborne invading troops. Official reaction to the speech among most of the major parties was negative, and even the Swedish army opposed the suggestion, seeing nuclear weapons procurement for the air force as potentially detracting from its influence and budget. Garris, *Sweden and the Spread of Nuclear Weapons,* p. 92.

43. Ibid., pp. 92, 102–4.

44. Agrell, "The Bomb That Never Was," pp. 161–62.

45. Garris, *Sweden and the Spread of Nuclear Weapons,* p. 261.

46. Johansson, "Sweden's Abortive Nuclear Weapons Program," p. 33. Opponents of nuclear weapons acquisition also received assurances from the government that FOA's research would be carefully monitored. Reiss, *Without the Bomb,* p. 59.

47. U.S. Department of State, Bureau of Intelligence and Research, "Swedish Government Initiates Nuclear Weapons Research," *Intelligence Report* no. 8223, February 12, 1960, p. 3.

48. Thomas B. Johansson ("Sweden's Abortive Nuclear Weapons Project," p. 32) summarized FOA's research at that time:

> Leading cabinet members permitted the military to continue with its weapons program and covertly provided increasingly larger funds for the purpose. The work included design work on a battery-operated pulsed-neutron source for initiating the chain reaction in a nuclear explosion, safety catches, fast explosion lenses, methods for simultaneous initiation of conventional explosives, and many other technical details for weapons design. In 1958 the cabinet also secretly approved the construction of a laboratory for separating small amounts of plutonium from nuclear fuel at Ursvik, outside of Stockholm. The military equipment firm AB Bofors began looking into the details of industrial manufacturing of nuclear weapons. Various studies were done on possible weapons delivery systems.

49. Although Sweden had adequate natural uranium sources to team with heavy water for its reactors, it lacked plutonium for its military program. To generate the Pu-239 necessary for weapons, the government relied on secret plans designated the "L-Program." The L-Program envisioned extracting twenty to twenty-five kilograms of weapons-grade plutonium per year from the Agesta plant by 1962, enough for a few fission weapon cores. The Marviken plant would be capable of producing forty to eighty kilograms of plutonium per year, enough for ten tactical nuclear weapons. Although reprocessing plutonium from spent uranium was economically unjustified for use as commercial fuel at that time, AB Atomenergi launched a study of reprocessing "on a scale corresponding to what Agesta, Marviken, and perhaps one more research reactor could produce—a scale which fitted well with the military's estimates of Sweden's nuclear weapons requirements" (Cole, *Neutralité du jour,* p. 386). Parliament's decision to defer a decision on the bomb and expand "defensive research" did not derail the L-Program. Larsson, "The History of the Swedish Atom Bomb"; Cole, *Neutralité du jour,* p. 386.

50. Agrell, "The Bomb That Never Was," p. 167.

51. Cole, *Neutralité du jour,* p. 386.

52. FOA recognized early that Marviken would not be an ideal facility, and, as feared, the project became delayed, increasingly expensive, and technologically complicated. Power output based on natural uranium proved unacceptably low, control problems surfaced, and plant safety standards were made difficult because the project was not subject to international cooperation and the sharing of technical data and technological improvements. Ibid.

53. By 1961, the inability of the civilian program to stay on budget was fraying the military consensus over the wisdom of deriving nuclear weapons material from the civilian program and whether conventional defense modernization was suffering because of the costs of the nuclear program. The military had committed itself to pursuing the nuclear weapons program within the existing defense budgets and believed that, with an anticipated 2.5 percent budgetary increase for new technology decided in 1958, its research into the weapons program would stay within budget. By 1961, however, the cost of the domestic program had risen rapidly, and the military began to consider plans for a reactor dedicated to plutonium production. Under these budgetary constraints, the trade-off between nuclear weapons research and conventional defense modernization began to move the military toward the goal of overall modernization of existing forces and away from its enthusiasm for nuclear weapons.

54. Jasper, *Nuclear Politics,* p. 67. Swedish power industry representatives frequently visited their American counterparts in the early 1960s to keep track of light water developments. Interview data, Stockholm, September 10, 1992.

55. Irving C. Bupp and Jean-Claude Derian, *Light Water* (New York: Basic Books, 1978), pp. 64–65.

56. Garris, *Sweden and the Spread of Nuclear Weapons,* p. 290.

57. Interview data, Stockholm, September 9, 1992. Glenn Seaborg, chair of the U.S. AEC, for example, recalled a specific conversation in the summer of 1962 with Sweden's Prime Minister Tage Erlander in which Erlander expressed his doubt about the natural uranium approach. Following AEC reductions in the cost of enriched uranium, Dr. Jan Rydberg, FOA's research director, visited Seaborg to discuss the changing economics of nuclear power. Glenn Seaborg, "Travels in the New World," Washington, DC, 1972, pp. 222–24.

58. O. Gimstedt, "Three Decades of Nuclear Power Development in Sweden," in *International Conference on Nuclear Power Experience* (Vienna: IAEA, 1983), pp. 133–34.

59. Ibid.

60. Interview data, Stockholm, September 9, 1992; Interview data, Stockholm, September 11, 1992.

61. Agrell, "The Bomb That Never Was."

62. Garris, *Sweden and the Spread of Nuclear Weapons,* p. 358.

63. U.S. Department of State, *Report of the Bureau of Intelligence and Research,* February 12, 1960, cited in Johansson, *Sweden's Abortive Nuclear Weapons Program,* p. 32.

64. See for example, ibid.; Secretary of Defense Memorandum from Robert

McNamara to President John Kennedy, "The Diffusion of Nuclear Weapons With and Without a Test Ban Treaty," Washington, DC, February 12, 1963.

65. Quester, *The Politics of Nuclear Nonproliferation,* p. 125.

66. Interview data, Washington, DC, June 4, 1992.

67. Reiss, *Without the Bomb,* p. 247. See also Garris, *Sweden and the Spread of Nuclear Weapons,* pp. 388–89.

68. Reiss, *Without the Bomb,* pp. 351–52. This restriction also would have applied to the Marviken facility had it become operational.

69. Garris, *Sweden and the Spread of Nuclear Weapons,* pp. 388–89.

70. Prawitz, "Sweden–A Non-nuclear Weapon State," p. 64.

71. Wilhelm Agrell's analysis stresses the growing divergences within the military organizations over the wisdom of pursuing nuclear weapons at the cost of overall military modernization. During the early 1960s, he claims, nuclear weapons procurement had lost clear support within the military and its survival was in doubt. Agrell, "The Bomb That Never Was."

72. Reiss, *Without the Bomb,* p. 64. "In 1957 nearly 40 percent of the Swedish people favored the acquisition of nuclear weapons, with 36 percent opposed. By 1967 those in favor fell below 17 percent while the opposition nearly doubled to 69 percent" (Cole, *Neutralité du jour,* p. 408).

73. Reiss, *Without the Bomb,* pp. 251–53. Clive Archer describes a phenomenon he calls the "Nordic balance," that is, "the desire of Nordic governments to give consideration to the security policy of their immediate neighbors when fashioning their own." Often the policy was to restrain military postures to reassure the Soviet Union in the expectation that the Soviets would reciprocate the restraint. "Nordic Security," *Contemporary Review* 243, no. 1411 (August 1983): 60–61.

74. During the 1950s, America's strategic nuclear arsenal expanded from a few weapons to more than 1,600 missiles, and its tactical nuclear warheads deployed in Europe totaled some 7,000 by the time of the Kennedy administration. The effect was to diminish the deterrent and war-fighting value of a handful of Swedish tactical nuclear weapons in a scenario involving widespread warfare in Europe. Later the Kennedy administration's strengthening of conventional defense in Europe further weakened the justification for a small independent Swedish nuclear force.

75. See Garris, *Sweden and the Spread of Nuclear Weapons,* p. 411. Thomas Johansson concludes, "It is questionable if the outcome of events in the later 1950s would have been the same if weapons could have been produced in a short time" ("Sweden's Abortive Nuclear Weapons Project," p. 34).

Chapter 4

1. In a February 1949 National Security Council report, forty-one countries recommended the establishment of a system of export controls on U.S. trade with China. See "Note by the Executive Secretary of the National Security Council (Souers), on the United States Policy Regarding Trade with China," February 28, 1949, *FRUS 1949,* vol. 9, pp. 826–34.

2. U. S. Congress, House, *Mutual Defense Assistance Control Act of 1951 (Battle Act): Hearings before the Committee on Foreign Relations,* 82d Cong., 1st sess.,

(1951), pp. 31–32 (Statement of Loring K. Macy, deputy director, Office of International Trade, Department of Commerce).

3. See D. Grant Seabolt, "United States Technology Exports to the People's Republic of China: Current Developments in Law and Policy," *Texas International Law Journal* 19, no. 3 (summer 1984): 599–600; Paul M. Evans, "Caging the Dragon: Post-War Economic Sanctions Against the People's Republic of China," in *The Utility of International Economic Sanctions,* ed. David Leyton-Brown (New York: St. Martin's Press, 1987), pp. 59–86.

4. COCOM—which was soon to include Japan and most of the NATO allies—coordinated the efforts of member countries to block the export of strategic commodities to communist nations. By March 1950 COCOM partners of the United States had agreed to apply the same export controls to China that they applied to the Soviet Union. In 1952 COCOM expanded the list of controls applicable to China. Within a year the China embargo list contained over four hundred categories of proscribed items, about twice the number on the Soviet list. Jing-dong Yuan, "Between Economic Warfare and Strategic Embargo: U.S.-U.K. Conflicts over Export Controls on the PRC, 1949–1957," *Issues and Studies* 30, no. 3 (March 1994): 80–86.

5. See "Report Prepared by the Economic Cooperation Administration," *FRUS 1951* 7 (February 1951): 1907–10.

6. See, for example, "Telegram from the Department of State to the Permanent Representative at the North Atlantic Council," *FRUS 1955–57* 10 (October 1, 1955): 255–56.

7. For a report of British and French dissatisfaction with stringent controls on China, see "Telegram from the Office of the Permanent Representative at the North Atlantic Council to the Department of State," *FRUS 1955–57* 10 (October 6, 1955): 259–62.

8. U.S. Congress, Senate, Committee on Foreign Relations, *U.S. Policy With Respect to Mainland China: Hearings before the Committee on Foreign Relations,* 89th Cong., 2d sess., 1966, p. 336–37. (Statement of Professor Alexander Eckstein.)

9. Evans, "Caging the Dragon," pp. 57–58.

10. Ibid., p. 59. The list of nonstrategic goods announced by the White House in June 1971 contained forty-seven categories of industrial and consumer products. The result was to bring U.S. limits on nonstrategic exports to China more in line with the restrictions imposed against the Soviet Union at that time. In addition, the U.S. government expedited visas for Chinese visitors, relaxed currency controls to permit China to pay for U.S. products in dollars, permitted American oil companies abroad to refuel most Chinese ships, and allowed aircraft and American ships to carry Chinese cargo under certain conditions.

11. U.S. Congress, House, Committee on Foreign Relations, *United States-China Relations: A Strategy for the Future: Hearings before the Committee on Foreign Relations, Subcommittee on Asian and Pacific Affairs,* 91st Cong., 2d sess., 1970, p. 290 (statement of Marshall Green, assistant secretary of state for East Asian and Pacific Affairs).

12. Shanghai Joint Communiqué, *Weekly Compiled Presidential Documents,* 8 (February 28, 1972): 473.

13. During the 1970s the United States accounted for only 3 percent of China's foreign trade. After three years of rapid growth following the resumption of commercial relations, U.S. exports to China actually declined during the 1974–77 period, and two-way trade did not surpass $1 billion until formal diplomatic recognition on January 1, 1979. James Tsao, *China's Development Strategies and Foreign Trade* (Lexington, MA: Lexington Books, 1987), p. 92. Several factors constrained bilateral trade. Technology restrictions limited trade to nonstrategic items such as agriculture and basic commodity and industrial goods. China's increasing grain production slowed U.S. agricultural exports. In the energy production equipment sector, China already had established relations with suppliers in Japan and Europe before the entry of U.S. business. In the area of low-to-medium technology, China's efforts to develop domestic suppliers as a part of its self-reliance policy limited U.S. export potential. Furthermore, China remained committed to maintaining a trade surplus through limiting purchases from foreign suppliers. See Sutter, *The China Quandary,* p. 129; Kim Woodward, *The International Energy Relations of China* (Stanford, CA: Stanford University Press, 1980), p. 36.

14. *Selected Works of Mao Zedong,* vol. 4 (Peking: People's Publishing House, 1968), p. 417.

15. Carol Lee Hamrin, "The Impact of Politics on China's Modernization," in *U.S.-China Trade: Problems and Prospects,* ed. Eugene Lawson (New York: Praeger, 1988), p. 63–64.

16. The PRC's first five-year economic plan (1953–57) incorporated the Soviet (Stalinist) model by calling for the collectivization of agriculture, the development of raw materials and capital industries, and reduced investment in consumer goods, agricultural production, and social overhead, all under a centralized plan. Harry Harding, *China's Second Revolution* (Washington, DC: Brookings Institution, 1987), p. 15. The plan and its immediate successor produced a high rate of growth in industrial production in heavy industries at the expense of agriculture. China completed the collectivization of agriculture and industry during these years. By 1957 private economic activity accounted for a scant 2 to 3 percent of national output. Robert Michael Field, "The Growth of China's Economy, 1949–85, in *U.S.-China Trade: Problems and Prospects* (New York: Praeger, 1988), p. 42.

17. Tsao, *China's Development Strategies,* p. 84.

18. China also eschewed foreign loans and investment and limited its scientific and educational exchanges. Harding, *China's Second Revolution,* p. 23.

19. Ibid., p. 33. T. David McDonald notes that "while some aspects of Chinese society clearly reflect a high degree of technical skill (China had nuclear weapons by 1968), the overall technological level is 30 years behind that of the developed West." McDonald attributes the problem not only to isolation but to the failure to integrate new technology into improved production. T. David McDonald, *The Technological Transformation of China* (Washington, DC: National Defense University Press, 1990), p. xxii.

20. Harding, *China's Second Revolution,* pp. 136–49.

21. Political division in China made the future course of its foreign policy unclear. Harry Harding describes Chinese internal politics in this era as a struggle

among three groups: the revolutionary Maoists, the restorationists, and the reformers. These groups struggled for control of China's destiny in the late 1970s and early 1980s. Harding, *China's Second Revolution,* pp. 48–49.

22. Sutter, *The China Quandary,* p. 131.

23. *Beijing Review* (December 29, 1978): 6–16, as quoted in Samuel Ho and Ralph Huenemann, *China's Open Door Policy: The Quest for Foreign Technology and Capital* (Vancouver: University of British Columbia Press, 1984), p. 2.

24. Chen Qiwei, "Why Is China Opening to the Outside?" *Beijing Review* (April 1, 1985): 18–22.

25. Tsao, *China's Development Strategies,* p. 96.

26. Zbigniew Brzezinski, *Power and Principle: Memoirs of the National Security Advisor 1977–1981* (New York: Farrar, Strauss and Giroux, 1983), p. 403.

27. Cyrus Vance, *Hard Choices: Critical Years in American Foreign Policy* (New York: Simon and Schuster, 1983), p. 76.

28. Michael Oksenberg, "A Decade of Sino-American Relations," *Foreign Affairs* 61, no. 1 (1982): 178.

29. Brzezinski, *Power and Principle,* p. 203.

30. Ibid.

31. Oksenberg, "Sino-American Relations," p. 185.

32. Brzezinski, *Power and Principle,* p. 204.

33. Ibid., p. 214.

34. Although most U.S. legislators accepted Carter's decision to recognize the mainland government and demote Taiwan's diplomatic status, the decision had to survive several pro-Taiwanese challenges. In January 1979, Republican Senator Barry Goldwater of Arizona led twenty-three congressional members in a suit challenging the president's termination of the U.S.-Taiwan Defense Treaty on constitutional grounds, claiming only Congress could abrogate a treaty. This challenge was put to rest when the U.S. Supreme Court declined to hear the case. Congress also passed the Taiwan Relations Act, which ensured close "semi-sovereign" relations between the U.S. and Taiwan. Carter reluctantly signed the act in April. Joseph Mortellaro, "Normalization and Subsequent Sino-American Economic Relations," *Asian Profile* 13 (1985): 292.

35. These Congressional requirements are discussed at length in chapter 5.

36. "Chinese Trade Pact is Sent to Congress," *New York Times,* October 24, 1979, p. 1.

37. Tsao, *China's Development Strategy,* p. 96.

38. The analytic foundations for departing from the policy of evenhandedness preceded the actual departure by several years. Michael Pillsbury, writing in 1975, argued: "We should modify the specious policy of evenhandedness which now governs exports of advanced defense technology. The same restrictions should not apply to both the Soviet Union and China. China is not nearly as large a security threat to us as the Soviet Union" ("U.S.-Chinese Military Ties?" *Foreign Policy,* no. 20 [fall 1975]: 63–64). Others have argued that the U.S. government began weighing the possibility of favoring the PRC with advanced technology as part of limited military cooperation beginning in 1972. See, for example, U.S. Congress, House, Committee on Foreign Relations, *United States and the People's Republic*

of China: Issues for the 1980s; Hearings before the Subcommittee on Asian and Pacific Affairs, 96th Cong. 2d sess., 1980, p. 97 (statement of Banning Garrett).

39. Mondale further pledged to provide China with U.S. Export-Import Bank financing of up to $2 billion over the next five years, to submit to Congress the previously negotiated Sino-American trade agreement, and to obtain congressional action that would provide investment guarantees of the Overseas Private Investment Corporation for U.S. investors in China. Tan Qingshan, *The Making of U.S. China Policy* (Boulder, CO: Lynne Rienner Publishers, 1992), p. 7, n. 5.

40. A. Doak Barnett, *China's Economy in Global Perspective* (Washington, DC: Brookings, 1981), p. 553; Stephen Barber, "Carter's Rude Awakening," *Far Eastern Economic Review* 107, no. 3 (January 18, 1980): 10–11.

41. In 1981, China began to acquire certain military equipment, including communication and deciphering technology. By 1983 military equipment purchases reached $71.7 million. Madelyn C. Ross, "Export Controls: Where China Fits In," *China Business Review* 11, no. 3 (May–June 1984): 58.

42. U.S. Congress, House, *Hearings before the Subcommittee on Asian and Pacific Affairs,* 96th Cong., 2d sess., 1980, pp. 1–3.

43. See "New Guidelines Set For Exports to China," *Business America* (October 6, 1980): 20.

44. Oksenberg, "Sino-American Relations," p. 192.

45. See U.S. International Trade Commission, *29th Quarterly Report to Congress and the Trade Policy Committee on Trade Between the U.S. and the Non-Market Countries During 1981* (Washington, DC: International Trade Commission, 1982), pp. 33–34. The United States also struck China from the list of countries denied arms sales effective December 14, 1981. License applications for commercial arms sales to China under the International Traffic in Arms Regulations were henceforth reviewed on a case-by-case basis.

46. By November, the Commerce Department had published new technical guidelines governing exports to China in seven areas considered most important to the PRC's modernization program, including computers, computerized instruments, microcircuits, electronic instruments, recording equipment, and oscilloscopes. The new guidelines raised the technical parameters of permissible exports in these commodity categories. "People's Republic of China; Export Control Policy; Placement in Country Group V," *Federal Register* 48 (1983): 53, 064–71.

47. In the first eleven months of 1984, bilateral high technology trade grew to $2.8 billion, up from $1 billion in 1983. *Asian Wall Street Journal Weekly* (December 31, 1984): 1.

48. U.S. Office of Technology Assessment, *Technology Transfer to China* (Washington, DC: Government Printing Office, July 1987), p. 206.

49. Banning Garrett and Bonnie Glaser, "From Nixon to Reagan: China's Changing Role in American Strategy," in *Eagle Resurgent?* ed. Kenneth A. Oye, Robert J. Licher, and Donald Rothchild (Boston, MA: Little, Brown, 1987), pp. 264–71.

50. Qingshan, *U.S. China Policy,* pp. 13–14.

51. Robert G. Sutter, "The Political Context of the Four Modernizations," in

U.S. Congress Joint Economic Committee, *China Under the Four Modernizations,* Part 1, 97th Cong., 2d sess., August 13, 1982, p. 97.

52. Bruce Cummings, "The Political Economy of China's Turn Outward," in *China and the World,* 2d ed., ed. Samuel Kim (Boulder, CO: Westview Press, 1989), p. 222.

53. Harding, *China's Second Revolution,* pp. 238–44.

54. In reporting the Seventh Five-Year Plan, Zhao Ziyang stressed a foreign policy based "on the merits of each case" and noted "closeness with or estrangement from other countries" would not be based on "their social systems or ideologies." Ibid.

55. Roger Sullivan, "The Nature and Implications of United States–China Trade Toward the Year 2000," in *China's Global Presence,* ed. David Lampton and Katherine Keyser (Washington, DC: American Enterprise Institute, 1988), p. 156 (emphasis added).

56. Kenneth Lieberthal, "Domestic Politics and Foreign Policy," in *China's Foreign Relations in the 1980s,* ed. Harry Harding (New Haven, CT: Yale University Press, 1984), p. 63.

57. Harry Harding, "China's Changing Roles in the Contemporary World," in *China's Foreign Relations in the 1980s,* ed. Harry Harding (New Haven, CT: Yale University Press, 1984), p. 194.

58. Shortly after the U.S.-PRC honeymoon of 1979–80, Ronald Reagan's election seriously strained relations. As a candidate, Reagan favored establishing official relations with Taiwan, and China suspected that as president, Reagan would pursue a two-China policy. Delays in license approvals for the promised export of U.S. high technology and the failure to agree on quotas for the import of Chinese textiles exacerbated these tensions. See, generally, Carol Lee Hamrin, "China Reassesses the Superpowers," *Pacific Affairs* 56, no. 2 (summer 1983): 209–25.

59. John Garver, "Peking's Soviet and American Policies: Toward Equidistance," *Issues and Studies* 24, no. 10 (October 1988): 56. Garver also noted that Chinese strategic cooperation with the United States had hurt its relations with certain third world nations, including India and North Korea.

60. Jonathan Pollack, "China and the Global Strategic Balance," in *China's Foreign Relations in the 1980s,* ed. Harry Harding (New Haven, CT: Yale University Press, 1984), pp. 81–82.

61. Donald Zagoria, "The Moscow-Beijing Détente," *Foreign Affairs* 61, no. 4 (spring 1983): 856.

62. Carol Lee Hamrin, *China and the Challenge of the Future* (Boulder, CO: Westview Press, 1990), p. 86.

63. Robert Sutter, "Realities of International Power and China's 'Interdependence' in Foreign Affairs," *Journal of Northeast Asian Studies* 3, no. 4 (winter 1984): 21. The importance China attaches to Western technology acquisition also can be seen in its refusal to curtail its level of Western technology imports during its foreign exchange crisis of 1984–85, judging such a policy too disruptive to its modernization goals. It chose instead to borrow from both public and commercial lenders to maintain import levels—a policy it refused to pursue in 1980–81 when its

technological reliance on the West was less pervasive. Albert Keidel, "China's Economy in the Year 2000," in *China's Global Presence* (Washington, DC: American Enterprise Institute for Public Policy Research, 1988), p. 78.

64. Paul Monen, "China, U.S. Set Further Arms Buy Talks," *Aviation Week and Space Technology* (June 11, 1984): 22–23.

65. The 1984 agreement opened up a vast arsenal of technology to China, including Hawk missiles, air defense radar and technology, long-range artillery ammunition, flight simulators, aircraft engines, and naval electronics. Nayan Chanda, "Towing the Peking Line," *Far Eastern Economic Review* (June 28, 1984): 12–13.

66. Richard Baum, "The Greening of the Revolution," *Asian Survey* 26, no. 1 (January 1986): 48.

67. Garver, "Peking's Soviet and American Policies," pp. 59–60.

68. Ibid.

69. See, for example, Robert Sutter, *Sino-Soviet Relations: Recent Improvements and Implications for the United States,* Library of Congress, Issue Brief, 86138, pp. 9,11.

70. For a discussion of the U.S. position, see Sutter, *The China Quandary,* pp. 111–26.

71. Nayan Chanda, "No Boats to China," *Far Eastern Economic Review* (May 30, 1985): 14–15; "Superpower Triangle," *Far Eastern Economic Review* (April 4, 1985): 17–18; "Ships that Pass . . . ," *Far Eastern Economic Review* (May 22, 1986): 32.

72. Roger W. Sullivan, "United States–China Trade Toward 2000," p. 159.

73. Harding, *China's Second Revolution,* p. 254.

74. As Donald S. Zagoria explained: "The proud, highly nationalistic Chinese were not suited to be the junior partner of the Americans any more than they were suited to be Moscow's junior partner in the 1950s" ("The Moscow-Beijing Détente," p. 860).

75. Yet, several years after the incident, much remains the same. China's modernization remains that country's chief priority and technology an important means. Moreover, American geopolitical interest also remains much the same. Richard Nixon commented on the relevance of China to U.S. interests:

> Even if we assume the Cold War is over . . . we still have a strong strategic interest in restoring a good relationship with the PRC. China is a nuclear power. Without Chinese cooperation, we cannot have an effective policy of nonproliferation of nuclear weapons and will have no leverage at all in trying to prevent the sale of missiles and other weapons to countries in trouble spots like the Middle East. Given Japan's status as an economic superpower, a strong and stable China with close ties to the United States is essential to balance the power of Japan and the Soviet Union in East Asia. China also has an indispensable role to play in the maintenance of peace and stability in the Asia-Pacific region, particularly on the Korean peninsula.

Cited in David M. Lampton, "America's China Policy: Developing a Fifth Strategy," in *The China Challenge: American Politics in East Asia,* ed. Frank J.

Macchiarola and Robert B. Oxnom, *Proceedings of the Academy of Political Science* 38, no. 2 (October 1991), p. 160.

76. See, for example, *Foreign Broadcast Information Service Daily Report,* September 8, 1982.

77. Winston Lord, "China and America: Beyond the Big Chill," *Foreign Affairs* 68, no. 4 (fall 1989): 9.

Chapter 5

1. That law prohibited loans or other buying or selling of bonds to countries in default to the United States. Congress passed the Johnson Act to show its displeasure with the Soviet Union's failure to negotiate repayment of czarist debts. In 1948, however, Congress amended the act to include East Germany and Czechoslovakia, countries within the Soviet orbit that had not joined the International Monetary Fund or World Bank. See Steven Dryden, "Banking and Credit," *The Post-Containment Handbook,* ed. Robert Cullen (Boulder, CO: Westview Press, 1990), p. 19.

2. In 1951, during the Korean War, Congress placed all communist countries in a high-tariff category. Unlike GATT members, Czechoslovakia did not receive most favored nation (MFN) tariff treatment. As a result of Congress's action, Czech exports were subject to the prohibitive Smoot-Hawley tariff levels of 1930.

3. Operationally, beginning with the onset of the Cold War, the United States controlled through government license the export of dual-use technologies (civilian goods and technologies with potential military applications). The United States coordinated its national security controls with other nations through COCOM. Member governments submitted license applications to export items above a certain technological threshold to COCOM for unanimous approval. COCOM members included Japan, Australia, and the North Atlantic Treaty Organization (NATO) countries (except Iceland).

4. Efforts to explore a more positive approach to the East in the 1970s as part of the policy of détente snagged on the issue of emigration. Specifically, Congress, wary of offering economic carrots to communist nations and sensitive to domestic pressures over the human rights conditions there, scuttled efforts to establish a new trading status for Eastern bloc countries when it passed the Jackson-Vanik amendment to the Trade Act of 1974. That amendment denied trade preferences to communist nations that restricted their citizens' right to emigrate. Although directed against the Soviet Union, Czech emigration laws under the communist regime similarly precluded it from preferential trade status. By the late 1970s, worsening East-West relations halted initiatives designed to improve trade and technology transfer relations. During the 1980s, the United States tightened technology transfer controls to the East, placing a heavy regulatory burden on U.S. exporters and straining relations with some COCOM allies. One exception to this trend was the liberalization of technology restrictions to the People's Republic of China discussed in chapter 4.

5. The emphasis on nonproliferation continued into the Clinton administration. President Clinton's secretary of state, Warren Christopher, remarked following

discussions with the foreign ministers of the leading industrial nations in 1993, "We stressed nonproliferation, because, in our view, nonproliferation is really the arms control issue of the 1990s." Press briefing by Secretary of State Warren Christopher and Secretary of Treasury Lloyd Benson, The Okura Hotel, Tokyo, Japan, July 7, 1993.

6. Secretary of State James Baker, "From Revolution to Democracy: Central and Eastern Europe in the New Europe," *U.S. Department of State Dispatch* (September 3, 1990): 12–13.

7. Ibid., p. 13.

8. Under U.S. law, the president has authority to grant annual waivers of the Jackson-Vanik restrictions to particular countries. Hungary, for example, qualified for such waivers beginning in 1978, and Czechoslovakia was granted a waiver in 1990. The waiver, if not disapproved by Congress, provides for annually renewable MFN treatment.

9. *"Czechoslovakia: From Revolution to Renaissance," U.S. Department of State Dispatch.* Statement of President George Bush, November 17, 1990.

10. Ibid.

11. Although the focus here is on bilateral incentives, multilateral support for Czech reform efforts also increased. IMF disbursements in 1991 totaled $1.3 billion, those from the Bank for Reconstruction and Development totaled $300 million, and disbursements from the European Community stood at $200 million. Ivan Szitek, "An Assessment: Czechoslovak Economic Reform in 1991," *Radio Free Europe/Radio Liberty Research Report* 1, no. 21 (May 1992): 46. In April 1992, the IMF made a $3.3 billion loan to the CSFR, a vote of confidence in its economic reforms. Sharon L. Wolchik, "The Politics of Eastern Europe's Move to the Market," *Current History* 91 (November 1992): 393.

12. On April 10, President Bush signed the proclamation extending MFN benefits to Czechoslovakia on a permanent basis. "President Signs Measure Extending Permanent MFN to Hungary, CSFR," *International Trade Reporter* (April 15, 1992): 700.

13. "Bush Signs Bill on MFN for Baltics, Permanent MFN for Hungary, CSFR," *International Trade Reporter* (December 11, 1991): 1820. The U.S. General Accounting Office estimated that granting MFN status to Czechoslovakia would reduce the weighted average U.S. tariff rate on dutiable products from 29.5 percent to an estimated 5.2 percent. See U.S. Congress, Senate, *Extension of Non-Discriminatory Treatment to Products of the Czech and Slovak Federal Republic,* 101st Cong., 2d sess., January 14, 1991, pp. 5–6.

14. "President Signs Measure," p. 700.

15. "CSFR's Imports from the U.S. Grew 25 Percent as Exports Jump 75 Percent," *International Trade Reporter* (December 23, 1992): 2196. Czechoslovakia's largest export to the United States was woolen textiles, followed by bearings and tires, glass products, shoes, tractors, clothing, jewelry, steel, and fittings. Its major imports from the United States were cotton, data processing machines, copper, machinery, and electrical and telecommunications equipment. "CSFR Seeks to Expand Trade, Investment Ties With United States," *International Trade Reporter* (February 19, 1992): 322.

16. Ibid.

17. Included in these items were agricultural hops from Czechoslovakia, which accounted for $7.035 million in imports to the United States in 1991. "USTR Adds 83 Eastern European Products to GSP List Resulting From Special Review," *International Trade Reporter* (June 17, 1992): 1053.

18. "U.S.-C.S.F.R. Bilateral Agreement on Investments to Take Force December 19," *International Trade Reporter* (December 9, 1993): 2105.

19. "U.S. Will Continue Providing Aid to Divided CSFR, Official Says," *International Trade Reporter* (August 5, 1992): 1352.

20. See Richard T. Cupitt, "Export Controls: The Perspective of the Czech and Slovak Federal Republic," in *International Cooperation on Nonproliferation Export Controls,* ed. Gary K. Bertsch, Richard T. Cupitt and Steven Elliott-Gower (Ann Arbor: University of Michigan Press, 1994), pp. 87–88.

21. The criteria for favorable consideration status included: (1) a high-level assurance that the items would not be used for other than the stated end use; (2) government-issued and enforced assurances about the end use and end user; (3) a legislative framework for export licensing and enforcement; (4) prelicense and postshipment checks in coordination with U.S. or international officials; (5) procedures against illegal reexports; (6) recognized enforcement and investigation practices with sanctions against violators; and (7) cooperation with U.S. officials in enforcement matters. U.S. Department of Commerce, *Export Administration Report* (Washington, D.C. Government Printing Office, 1991), pp. 15–16.

22. See, "COCOM De-Proscribes Hungary, Loosens Poland and Czechoslovakia Controls," *Export Control News* (February 27, 1992): 3.

23. The process of deproscription was slowed by the split between the Czech and Slovak Republics at the end of 1992. U.S. officials believed, however, that full deproscription for the Czech Republic was only a matter of time. Allen Wendt, "U.S. Export Controls in a Changing Global Environment," *U.S. Department of State Dispatch* (July 1, 1991): 480–82. See also ibid. Czech officials expressed the same opinion. In 1992, Deputy Foreign Trade Minister Jiri Brabec remarked, "We have received a commitment that we will be removed from the list." Because of the imminent split with Slovakia, he expected the decision to be implemented some time in 1993. "U.S. Welcomes COCOM Decision to Relax Controls on High-Tech Exports to Hungary," *International Trade Reporter* (May 6, 1992): 791. The CSFR formally applied to COCOM for removal from the list of proscribed countries in December 1992, just before the split between the Czech and Slovak Republics into two nations. In addition to issues related to separation, other factors delayed full deproscription for the Czech Republic. These matters included inadequate technical means for implementing safeguards (primarily computers and trained personnel) and inadequate sanctions and enforcement procedures. Olga Fantova, *Czech and Slovak Arms Exports: Policy Choices in Times of Economic Change,* master's thesis, University of Georgia, 1993, pp. 40–41. The Czech Republic was deproscribed in January 1994.

24. "President Bush December 6 Lifted U.S. Arms Embargoes," *International Trade Reporter* (December 11, 1991): 1827.

25. "Arms Conversion Discussed with U.S. Official," Ceskoslovensky Rozhlas

Radio Network, July 17, 1991, in *East Europe,* FBIS-EEU-91–139 (July 19, 1991): 15.

26. See "Dobrovsky Welcomes Lifting of U.S. Arms Embargo," CSTK, December 10, 1991, in *East Europe,* FBIS-EEU-91–239 (December 12, 1991): 8.

27. Generally this requires a system whereby the exporter certifies and the importer verifies the end use and end user of any sensitive technology leaving the country.

28. In approving MFN treatment for Czechoslovakia, the House Ways and Means Committee report described the revolutionary political and economic changes that the country had undergone and concluded: "Because the Committee believes that the United States should support and reward those changes, the Committee strongly urges expeditious enactment of H.J. Res. 649 and the extension of MFN treatment to the goods in Czechoslovakia." U.S. House of Representatives, *Approval of Extension of Most-Favored-Nation Treatment to Czechoslovakia,* 101st Cong., 2d sess., November 15, 1990, p.1.

29. Milan Svek, "Czechoslovakia's Velvet Divorce," *Current History* 91 (November 1992): 376.

30. Ibid.

31. Francis T. Miko, "Parliamentary Development in the Czech and Slovak Federal Republic," *CRS Review* (July 1991): 35–37.

32. Cupitt, "Export Controls," p. 89.

33. Czechoslovakia was partially successful in reorienting its trade: the share of exports to countries with market economies increased from 52.6 percent in 1990 to 60.7 percent in 1991. Szitek, "An Assessment," p. 46. By 1991, this reorientation and the institution of hard currency exchange with former CMEA members meant that over 95 percent of the CSFR's payments were in hard currency. The country ended that year with a $900 million trade surplus. Wolchik, "Eastern Europe's Move to Market," p. 393.

34. In the initial phase of economic reform, the government liberalized prices, subjected wages and the budget to tight controls and made the crown, the country's currency, internally convertible, which allowed businesses to buy foreign currency at the official exchange rate. Tax reform and privatization of small, then large, firms were the next immediate steps undertaken by the government. Svec, "Czechoslovakia's Velvet Divorce," p. 377.

35. In moving toward a market economy and reorienting its economic focus under the Federal government's "Scenario for Economic Reform," the gross domestic product fell by 13.4 percent in 1991 and contracted again in 1992 to a lesser extent. Unemployment, which was near zero at the beginning of 1991, reached 6.6 percent by year's end: 4.1 percent in the Czech Republic and 11.8 percent in the Slovak Republic. The different impact of reform on the two republics stemmed from the fact that Slovakia was much less economically developed than Czech lands before the coming of communism. Slovakian industrialization occurred during the communist period and reflected the distortions associated with Stalinist economic development. Economist Intelligence Unit, *Country Report-Czechoslovakia,* 1992; Szitek, "An Assessment," p. 48.

36. Rolf Alter, "New Challenges in Eastern Europe; Investment and Restructuring," *Intereconomics* 27 (1992): 16–19. Government officials envisioned an important role for foreign investors in privatizing and stimulating the economy. By June 1991, some four thousand joint ventures had been established, most of them in the Czech Republic. Wolchik, "Eastern Europe's Move to Market," p. 393.

37. "OECD Report Praises CSFR for Rapid Economic Progress," *International Trade Reporter* (January 8, 1992): 69.

38. Cupitt, "Export Controls," p. 89.

39. Jiri Pehe, ed., "Czechoslovakia in a New International Context," *Radio Free Europe/Radio Liberty Research Report* 1, no. 16 (April 1992): 30.

40. Milan Suchanek, "Nations Urged to Heed Example, End Arms Export," Radio Prague, January 26, in *East Europe,* FBIS-EEU-90–025 (February 6, 1990): 12–13.

41. During the communist era, decisions to export military or dual-use items were made at the discretion of the central planners and the Communist party. Western-style systems of licensing based on a legal framework were wholly unnecessary. At most, Czechoslovakia would have to request permission from the Soviet Union to export certain technologies made under Soviet license. On some occasions the Soviet Union would preempt a sale for foreign policy reasons, offering to buy the shipment at premium prices. See Cupitt, "Export Controls," p. 90.

42. After creating a new federal government in the autumn of 1990, the Federal Assembly of the CSFR passed Law 547/1990 on December 5 of that year. The statute, "On Dealing With Certain Kinds of Goods and Technologies and Control Thereof," took effect on February 1, 1991. The law empowered the Federal Foreign Trade Ministry to license the import and export of controlled goods and gave the Customs Administration of the CSFR (part of the Ministry of Finance) authority to inspect for compliance with the law and identify violators.

43. The Federal Assembly passed a second provision, Law 545/1990, amending the criminal code to create legal penalties, sanctions, and punishment for violating the country's new export control laws.

44. "Document on Arms Transfers Approved," CSTK, January 30, 1992, in *East Europe,* FBIS-EEU-92–021 (January 31, 1992): 4.

45. "No Objections to Total Ban on Chemical Weapons," *Svobodne Slovo,* October 25, 1990, p. 2, in *East Europe,* FBIS-EEU-90–212 (November 1, 1990): 18. In 1991, the CSFR became the first country to pass a list of chemical production facilities and submit a document about its protective antichemical agents for inspection to the international community. "List of Chemical Warfare Agents Producers Reported," *Mlada Fronta Dnes,* February 21, 1991, p. 2, in *East Europe,* FBIS-EEU-91–039 (February 27, 1991): 22; "CSFR Briefs Arms Forum on Antichemical Agents," Stanice Ceskoslovensko Radio, March 20, 1992, in *East Europe,* FBIS-EEU-92–057 (March 24, 1992): 3.

46. "U.S., Other Nations Reach Agreement on Restricting Nuclear Weapons Exports," *International Trade Reporter* (March 11, 1992): 435.

47. "Czech Envoy Supports Global Nuclear Test Ban," CTK, January 11, 1991, in *East Europe,* FBIS-EEU-90–012 (January 17, 1991): 2.

48. "Cabinet Joins Arms Embargo, Addresses Reforms," CTK, July 11, 1991, in *East Europe,* FBIS-EEU-91–134 (July 12, 1991): 8.

49. Under these agreements, Czechoslovak forces would be reduced by 1,600 tanks, 2,309 armored vehicles, 2,335 artillery systems, and 24 combat airplanes, whether through destruction or export. These reductions were from an existing stock of 3,315 tanks, 4,503 combat vehicles, 3,485 artillery systems, and 446 fighter planes. The CSFR estimated that reduction of surplus armaments would cost 250 million crowns (almost $9 million). "National Assembly Approves Arms Agreements," CTK, March 19, 1991, in *East Europe,* FBIS-EEU-91–054 (March 20, 1991): 25.

50. The Czech Republic passed such a law in early 1994, although, at that time, Slovakia did not.

51. "Calfa Interviewed on Arms Trade, Policy," *Mlada Fronta Dnes,* March 5, 1992, p. 7, in *East Europe,* FBIS-EEU-92–047 (March 10, 1992): 11–14. See also Cupitt, "Export Controls," p. 92.

52. Under communist rule, only the foreign trade organization Omnipol (with a deputy foreign trade minister as its director) had the right to trade in arms. In contrast, under privatization, twenty-eight firms soon had permits to engage in arms trade. Ibid., p. 95.

53. A spokesman for Federal Minister of Foreign Affairs Egon Lansky conceded that the arms lobby had blocked restrictive arms trade legislation and constituted an obstacle to conversion. Prime Minister Calfa added, "The problem centers on regional impact and a lobby that was accustomed to a certain status and appears unable to tolerate the loss." "Calfa Interviewed on Arms Trade, Policy," p. 12.

54. Cupitt, "Export Controls," p. 94. At its peak in the mid-1980s, Czechoslovakia was the fifth leading arms exporter in the world (second only to the Soviet Union in Eastern Europe), with as many as 150,000 people employed directly in defense production—60 percent of those employees in the Slovak Republic—with an estimated 200,000 to 250,000 additional workers indirectly dependent on the arms industry for jobs. Czechoslovakia was a major manufacturer of tanks, armored personnel carriers, self-propelled artillery, jet trainers, small arms, ammunition, and electronics. Up to 78 percent of this production was exported, probably the highest percentage in the world. U.S. Congress, Senate, Committee on Governmental Affairs, Subcommittee on Investigations, *Conversion of Arms Industry in Central Europe,* report prepared by Steven Popper, 102 Cong., 2d sess., 1991, p. 29.

55. Cupitt, "Export Controls," p. 94. Cupitt notes that the demise of the Warsaw Treaty Organization and the political and economic changes that swept the region sharply diminished the demand for CSFR arms in its traditional markets. Global arms markets shrank 18 percent in 1989, and the demand for Czechoslovak tanks fell 90 percent between 1988 and 1990. Moreover, the end of the Cold War found neither East nor West very amenable to supporting arms buildups elsewhere, an attitude only heightened by events surrounding the Persian Gulf War.

Many third world markets were saturated with arms, and many of these clients were insolvent or required credit terms the CSFR could not provide. Markets for Czech mid-level military technology were limited, largely confined to niche markets in the Middle East or a developing nation engaged in a regional struggle. See *World Military Expenditures and Arms Transfers* (Washington, DC: Government Printing Office, 1989–90), p. 12; "Official on Production of Armaments," CTK, June 20, 1990, in *East Europe,* FBIS-EEU-90–121 (June 22, 1990): 20.

56. Oldrich Cerny, "Czechoslovakia: Problems with Conversion," in U.S. Cong., Senate, Committee on Government Affairs, Subcommittee on Investigations, *Conversion of Arms Industry in Central Europe,* 102 Cong., 2d sess., 1991.

57. James L. Graff, "Confronting a Tankless Task," *Time,* June 17, 1991, p. 42. Reduction in arms production and export was a particularly volatile issue in the Slovak Republic, especially central Slovakia. For example, plans for reducing state armaments production touched off strikes at the Dubnica Heavy Engineering Works in Slovakia, one of the enterprises not designated to receive government conversion support. "General Details Arms Production Phase-out," *Mlada Fronta,* in *East Europe,* FBIS-EEU-90–056 (March 22, 1990): 22.

58. Paulina Bern, "Conversion Slows Down as Czechs and Slovaks Part," *Radio Free Europe/Radio Liberty Research Project* 1, no. 32 (August 14, 1992): 38.

59. While the Slovak Republic was retreating from a federal policy of arms export restraint and defense conversion, the Czech Republic remained committed to substantial conversion over a six-year period. Czech conversion faced a much easier road for several reasons. First, Czech arms manufacturers were smaller in number of employees than Slovak producers (averaging 2,000 to 4,000 workers versus 16,000 to 18,000 in Slovakia). This smaller size facilitated restructuring and made it easier to improve communication, adopt more flexible production patterns, or, if need be, release workers into the labor force. Second, in contrast to Slovakia, where most firms are located in the Vah Valley, Czech arms manufacturers were not geographically concentrated. Third, Czech arms manufacturers had stronger in-house research and development departments than many of their Slovak counterparts did. Slovak production was based largely on Soviet manufacturing licenses, with little indigenous development. Relatedly, Czech export markets were more diverse owing to the relative high quality of some of their defense production, and thus they were less vulnerable to the loss of Warsaw Pact and CMEA markets. Many more Czech firms, therefore, had the ability, flexibility, and financial resources to shift production to civilian goods or find new export markets for arms. Even before conversion, Czech companies manufactured a wide assortment of civilian goods in related sectors, including hunting and sport guns, automobiles, trucks, auto parts, roller bearings, and others. The Czech situation allowed firms to more easily close or convert unprofitable defense plants while retaining profitable ones, that is, those able to export to the West. Czech arms manufacturers continued to produce handguns, jet aircraft trainers, and electronic systems—sometimes with the aid of Western partners. Fantova, *Czech and Slovak Arms Exports,* pp. 85–86. Regarding Western assistance in modernizing Czechoslovak defense, see "Military Cooperation Accord Signed with France," CSTK, April 13, 1992, in *East Europe,* FBIS-EEU-92–068 (April 8, 1992): 3; "Turning to Tanks to Fill the

Till," *Business Week* (July 12, 1993): 20; "Company Plans to Modernize T-72 Tank," *Mlada Fronta Dnes,* June 29, 1993, pp. 1–2, in *East Europe,* FBIS-EEU-93–126 (July 2, 1993): 11.

60. Ibid., p. 39, quoting Slovak Prime Minister Vladimir Meciar. In 1991, the Slovak Republic slowed the pace of converting arms production to civilian production. Its stated rationale was that the arms exports provided a profit for the republic and that slowing defense conversion would meet the needs of the people of the Slovak region. By 1992, Meciar had formed a new political party, the Movement for a Democratic Slovakia, that made continuation of subsidies to Slovak defense enterprises an important element of its party platform, a promise Meciar reiterated after his election as the prime minister of Slovakia.

61. The CSFR conversion efforts were beset by a host of problems, some of its own making, others beyond its control. Federal government conversion policy incorrectly assumed that most arms manufacturers were capable of moving toward civilian production without substantial government aid or intervention and that conversion funds were distributed to arms-producing plants without stipulations and a concrete conversion program for them to follow. Factors outside Czechoslovakia's control did not make the job of defense conversion any easier. Conversion problems worsened with world recession. Lack of economic dynamism in Europe at the time dampened enthusiasm for prospective joint ventures with CSFR partners or made the output of new ventures difficult to sell abroad.

62. For example, in 1991 U.S. Deputy Secretary of Defense Donald Atwood promised that the United States would prepare a list of American companies that would be willing to invest in Slovak firms if they were privatized. This promise fell short of offering direct aid to finance the process of privatization or conversion that some expected. "Small Arms Exports to Proposed," CTK, April 15, 1991, in *East Europe,* FBIS-EEU-91–074 (April 17, 1991): 10.

63. Graff, "Confronting a Tankless Task," p. 42. Indeed, as the arms export and conversion issues played out, many in the CSFR voiced skepticism regarding U.S. and Western intentions in attempting to discourage Czechoslovak arms sales. Some believed the Western powers intended to secure markets for themselves. Josef Baksay, a former Czechoslovak trade minister, warned that as Czechoslovak arms production fell, "leading industrial countries increased their production and replaced our deliveries." Bern, "Conversion Slows Down," p. 42.

64. Notably, the complete elimination of CSFR defense capability was never the U.S. goal. By 1992, the United States came to see the CSFR as a potential participant in NATO that would need to retain some defense capabilities compatible with the West.

65. Cupitt, "Export Controls," pp. 98–99. Other international norms and institutions have helped shape CSFR policies and have deflected the influence of domestic forces opposed to change. For example, the United Nations embargo on arms trade with Iraq and the EC embargo on arms sales to Yugoslavia also discouraged weapons sales. Likewise, the CSFR decision to sign the Treaty on Conventional Armed Forces in Europe, which required it to make dramatic cuts in major conventional weapons, including tanks, armored personnel vehicles, and planes, strengthened the country's conversion efforts.

Chapter 6

1. Alexander L. George, *Bridging The Gap: Theory and Practice in Foreign Policy* (Washington, DC: U.S. Institute of Peace, 1993), p. xxiv.

2. Ibid., p. xvii.

3. Ibid., pp. 117–18.

4. Ibid., pp. 117–41.

5. Thomas C. Schelling, *Arms and Influence* (New Haven, CT: Yale University Press, 1966), p. 123.

6. On confidence-building measures see, Jonathan Alford, *Confidence-building Measures in Europe: The Military Aspects,* Adelphi Paper no. 149 (London: International Institute for Strategic Studies, 1979); Johan Jorgen Holst, "Confidence-building: A Conceptual Framework," *Survival* 25, no. 1 (January/February 1983): 2–15; Stephen Larabee and Dietrich Stobbes, eds., *Confidence-building Measures in Europe* (New York: Institute for East-West Security Studies, 1983).

7. On this point see David Baldwin, "Inter-nation Influence Revisited," *Journal of Conflict Resolution* 15, no. 4 (December 1971): 477.

8. Michael Weisskopf, "Chinese Trade Issues Seen Snagging Schultz," *Washington Post,* January 31, 1983, Section A, p. 12.

9. Richard Nations, "Who's in Charge Here?," *Far Eastern Economic Review* 120, no. 14 (April 7, 1983): 28–29.

10. Banning Garrett and Bonnie Glaser, *War and Peace: The Views From Moscow and Beijing* (Berkeley, CA: Institute of International Studies, 1984), p. 90.

11. "Commerce, DoD Clash over Export Controls," *Electronic News,* vol. 29, no. 1435 (March 7, 1983): 6; Stanford L. Jacobs, "Small Firms Upset by Effort to Limit High-Tech Exports," *Wall Street Journal,* April 4, 1983, 19.

12. Chris Brown, "The Problem With Country Group P," *China Business Review* 9, no. 2 (March–April 1982): 21–22.

13. U.S. Central Intelligence Agency, Technology Transfer Assessment Center, "Soviet Requirements for Western Technology," Washington, DC, 1987. See also Lionel H. Olmer and William J. Long, "Setting Technology Export Thresholds," in *Law and Policy of Export Controls,* ed. Homer Moyer et al. (Washington, DC: American Bar Association Press, 1993), pp. 491–510.

14. Some have argued that influence attempts based on vague demands may be more successful than those based on specific demands. See Schelling, *Arms and Influence,* pp. 84–85; Robert Jervis, *The Logic of Images in International Relations* (Princeton, NJ: Princeton University Press, 1970), pp. 123–30; David Baldwin, "Thinking About Threats," pp. 75–76.

15. William G. Hyland, "The Sino-Soviet Conflict," in *The China Factor: Sino-American Relations and the Global Scene,* ed. Richard Solomon (Englewood Cliffs, NJ: Prentice-Hall, 1981), p. 147.

16. *Pravda,* March 9, 1980, reprinted in *Washington Post,* March 10, 1980, Section A, p. 16.

17. See, for example, David Leyton-Brown, ed., *The Utility of International Economic Sanctions* (London: Croom & Helm, 1987).

18. See Hufbauer, Schott, and Elliott, *Economic Sanctions Reconsidered,* chap. 5.

19. David Baldwin, *Economic Statecraft,* p. 371.

20. Ibid., chap. 7.

21. Ibid., p. 119.

22. If the donor's prices for the tied-aid goods exceed world prices, then the value of the aid incentive is reduced for the beneficiary and, other things being equal, the degree of policy concession that can be "purchased."

Chapter 7

1. Lijphart, "Comparative Politics and the Comparative Method," pp. 685–86.

2. See Thomas Friedman, "A Diplomatic Question: Embargo or Embrace," *New York Times,* September 4, 1994, Section E, p. 4.

3. Stein, *Why Nations Cooperate,* p. 14.

4. For a discussion of the reasons for the growth in nontariff barriers to trade, see Edward John Ray, "Changing Patterns of Protection: The Fall in Tariffs and the Rise in Non-Tariff Barriers," *Northwestern Journal of International Law and Business* 8 (1987): 286–326. See also Robert Baldwin, "U.S. Trade Policy Since World War II," in *The Structure and Evolution of Recent U.S. Trade Policy,* ed. Robert Baldwin and Anne Krueger (New York: Blackwell, 1990), p. 10.

5. "Hard-core" nontariff barriers (NTBs) represent a subgroup of all possible NTBs. They are the ones most likely to have significant restrictive effects. Hard-core NTBs include import prohibitions, quantitative restrictions, voluntary export restraints, variable levies, Multi Fiber Arrangement restrictions, and nonautomatic licensing. Examples of other NTBs that are excluded include technical barriers (including health and safety restrictions and standards), minimum pricing regulations, and the use of price investigations (for example, for countervailing and antidumping purposes) and price surveillance. Percentage of imports subject to NTBs measures the sum of the value of the U.S. import group affected by the NTBs, divided by the total value of U.S. imports in that group. Data on imports affected in 1986 are based on 1981 trade weights. Variations between 1982 and 1986 can therefore occur only if NTBs affect a different set of products or trading partners.

For empirical evidence of the growth in U.S. NTBs during the 1970s using a broader definition, see S. A. B. Page, "The Management of International Trade," in *Britain's Trade and Exchange Rate Policy,* ed. Robert Major (London: Heinemann, 1979), 164–99.

6. Axelrod and Keohane, "Achieving Cooperation Under Anarchy," pp. 227–32.

Appendix

1. For a similar application of the bargaining and exchange model to economic coercion, see Cheng-Tian Kuo, "Formal Models of Economic Statecraft," paper presented at the annual meeting of the International Studies Association, Acapulco, Mexico, March 24, 1993. See generally Charles A. Lave and James G. March, *An Introduction to Models in the Social Sciences* (New York: Harper & Row, 1975), chap. 5.

Bibliography

Agrell, Wilhelm. "The Bomb That Never Was: The Rise and Fall of the Swedish Nuclear Weapons Program." In *Arms Races: Technological and Political Dynamics*, edited by Nils Peter Gleditsch and Olan Njolstud. Oslo, Norway: International Peace Research Institute, 1990.

Alford, Jonathan. *Confidence-building Measures in Europe: The Military Aspects.* Adelphi Paper no. 149. London: International Institute for Strategic Studies, 1979.

Allison, Graham T. *Essence of Decision: Explaining the Cuban Missile Crisis.* Boston, MA: Little, Brown and Company, 1971.

Alter, Rolf. "New Challenges in Eastern Europe; Investment and Restructuring." *Intereconomics* 27 (1992): 16–19.

Archer, Clive. "Nordic Security." *Contemporary Review* 243, no. 1411 (August 1983): 57–63.

"Arms Conversion Discussed with U.S. Official." Ceskoslovensky Rozhlas Radio Network, July 17, 1991. In *East Europe,* FBIS-EEU-91–139, July 19, 1991, p. 5.

Axelrod, Robert. *The Evolution of Cooperation.* New York: Basic Books, 1984.

Axelrod, Robert, and Robert Keohane. "Achieving Cooperation Under Anarchy: Strategies and Institutions." *World Politics* 38, no. 1 (October 1985): 226–54.

Baker, James. "From Revolution to Democracy: Central and Eastern Europe in the New Europe." *U.S. Department of State Dispatch* (September 3, 1990): 12–13.

Baker, Steven J. *Commercial Nuclear Power and Nuclear Proliferation.* Peace Studies Occasional Paper no. 5, Cornell University, May 1975.

Baldwin, David. *Economic Statecraft.* Princeton, NJ: Princeton University Press, 1985.

Baldwin, David. "Power and Social Exchange." *American Political Science Review* 72, no. 4 (December 1978): 1229–42.

Baldwin, David. "Inter-nation Influence Revisited." *Journal of Conflict Resolution* 15, no. 4 (December 1971): 471–85.

Baldwin, David. "The Power of Positive Sanctions." *World Politics* 24, no. 1 (October 1971): 19–38.

Baldwin, David. "Thinking About Threats." *Journal of Conflict Resolution* 15, no. 1 (March 1971): 71–78.

Baldwin, David. *Economic Development and American Foreign Policy.* Chicago: University of Chicago Press, 1966.

Baldwin, Robert. "U.S. Trade Policy Since World War II." In *The Structure and Evolution of Recent U.S. Trade Policy,* edited by Robert Baldwin and Anne Krueger. New York: Blackwell, 1990.

Barber, James. "Economic Sanctions as a Policy Instrument." *International Affairs* 55, no. 3 (July 1979): 367–84.

Barber, Steven. "Carter's Rude Awakening." *Far Eastern Economic Review* 107 (January 18, 1980): 10–11.

Barnett, A. Doak. *China's Economy in Global Perspective.* Washington, DC: Brookings, 1981.

Baum, Richard. "The Greening of the Revolution." *Asian Survey* 26, no. 1 (January 1986): 30–53.

Bern, Paulina. "Conversion Slows Down as Czechs and Slovaks Part." *Radio Free Europe/Radio Liberty Research Project* 1 (August 14, 1992): 38.

Brecher, Michael. *Decisions in Israel's Foreign Policy.* New Haven, CT: Yale University Press, 1974.

Brown, Chris. "The Problem With Country Group P." *China Business Review* 9, no. 2 (March–April 1982): 21–22.

Brzezinski, Zbigniew. *Power and Principle: Memoirs of the National Security Advisor 1977–1981.* New York: Farrar, Strauss, and Giroux, 1983.

Bupp, Irving C., and Jean-Claude Derian. *Light Water.* New York: Basic Books, 1978.

Burn, Duncan. *The Political Economy of Nuclear Energy.* London: Institute of Economic Affairs, 1967.

"Bush Signs Bill on MFN for Baltics, Permanent MFN for Hungary, CSFR." *International Trade Reporter* (December 11, 1991): 1820.

"Cabinet Joins Arms Embargo, Addresses Reforms," CTK, July 11, 1991. In *East Europe,* FBIS-EEU-91-134, July 12, 1991, p. 8.

"Calfa Interviewed on Arms Trade, Policy," *Mlada Fronta Dnes,* March 5, 1992, p. 7. In *East Europe,* FBIS-EEU-92-047, March 10, 1992, pp. 11–14.

Chanda, Nayan. "No Boats to China." *Far Eastern Economic Review* (May 30, 1995): 14–15.

Chanda, Nayan. "Ships that Pass . . ." *Far Eastern Economic Review* (May 22, 1986): 32.

Chanda, Nayan. "Superpower Triangle." *Far Eastern Economic Review* (April 4, 1985): 17–18.

Chanda, Nayan. "Towing the Peking Line." *Far Eastern Economic Review* (June 28, 1984): 12–13.

"Chinese Trade Pact is Sent to Congress." *New York Times,* October 24, 1979, Section A, p. 1.

Claude, Inis, Jr. *Power and International Relations.* New York: Random House, 1962.

Clawson, Patrick. *How Has Saddam Hussein Survived?* Washington, DC: National Defense University, 1993.

"COCOM De-Proscribes Hungary, Loosens Poland and Czechoslovakia Controls." *Export Control News* (February 27, 1992): 3.

Cohen, Benjamin. "The Political Economy of International Trade." *International Organization* 44, no. 2 (spring 1990): 261–81.

Cole, Paul A. *Neutralité du jour.* Ph.D. diss., Johns Hopkins University, 1990.

"Commerce, DoD Clash Over Export Controls." *Electronic News* 29, no. 1435 (March 7, 1983): 6.

"Company Plans to Modernize T-72 Tank," *Mlada Fronta Dnes,* June 29, 1993, pp. 1–2. In *East Europe,* FBIS-EEU-93–126, July 2, 1993, p. 11.

Conybeare, John. *Trade Wars.* New York: Columbia University Press, 1987.

Cowhey, Peter F. "'States' and 'Politics' in American Foreign Policy." In *International Trade Policies,* edited by John S. Odell and Thomas D. Willet. Ann Arbor: University of Michigan Press, 1993.

"CSFR Briefs Arms Forum on Antichemical Agents," Stanice Ceskoslovensko Radio, March 20, 1992. In *East Europe,* FBIS-EEU-92–057, March 24, 1992, p. 3.

"CSFR Seeks to Expand Trade, Investment Ties With United States." *International Trade Reporter* (February 19, 1992): 322.

"CSFR's Imports from the U.S. Grew 25 Percent as Exports Jump 75 Percent." *International Trade Reporter* (December 23, 1992): 2196.

Cummings, Bruce. "The Political Economy of China's Turn Outward." In *China and the World, 2d ed.,* edited by Samuel Kim. Boulder, CO: Westview Press, 1989.

Cupitt, Richard T. "Export Controls: The Perspective of the Czech and Slovak Federal Republic." In *International Cooperation on Nonproliferation Export Controls,* edited by Gary T. Bertsch, Richard T. Cupitt, and Stephen Elliott-Gower. Ann Arbor: University of Michigan Press, 1994.

"Czech Envoy Supports Global Nuclear Test Ban," CTK, January 11, 1991. In *East Europe,* FBIS-EEU-90–012, January 17, 1991, p. 2.

Dahl, Robert A. *Pluralist Democracy in the United States: Conflict and Consent.* Chicago: Rand McNally, 1967.

Daoudi, M. S., and M. S. Dajani. *Economic Sanctions: Ideals and Experience.* London: Routledge & Kegan Paul, 1983.

Darley, John M., Sam Glucksberg, and Ronald A. Kinchla. *Psychology,* 4th ed. Englewood Cliffs, NJ: Prentice Hall, 1984.

DelSesto, Steven L. *Science, Politics and Controversy: Civilian Power in the United States 1946–1974.* Boulder, CO: Westview Press, 1987.

Dessler, David. "What's at Stake in the Agent-Structure Debate." *International Organization* 43, no. 3 (summer 1989): 441–73.

"Dobrovsky Welcomes Lifting of U.S. Arms Embargo," CSTK, December 10, 1991. In *East Europe,* FBIS-EEU-91–239, December 12, 1991, p. 8.

"Document on Arms Transfers Approved," CSTK, January 30, 1992. In *East Europe,* FBIS-EEU-92–021, January 31, 1992, p. 4.

Doxey, Margaret. "International Sanctions: A Framework for Analysis with Special Reference to the U.N. and South Africa." *International Organization* 26, no. 3 (summer 1972): 527–50.

Dryden, Steven. "Banking and Credit." In *The Post-Containment Handbook,* edited by Robert Cullen. Boulder, CO: Westview Press, 1990.

Economist Intelligence Unit, *Country Report—Czechoslovakia,* 1992.

Eisenhower, Dwight D. *Public Papers of the Presidents of the United States: Dwight D. Eisenhower, 1953–57,* 8 vols. Washington, DC: Government Printing Office, 1953–57.

Eklund, Sigmund. "Reliable Supply: Respecting the 'Rules of the Game.'" In *Atoms for Peace: An Analysis After Thirty Years,* edited by Joseph F. Pilat, Robert E. Pendley, and Charles K. Ebinger. Boulder, CO: Westview Press, 1983.

Evans, Paul M. "Caging the Dragon: Post-War Economic Sanctions Against the People's Republic of China." In *The Utility of International Economic Sanctions,* edited by David Leyton-Brown. New York: St. Martin's Press, 1987.

Fantova, Olga. *Czech and Slovak Arms Exports: Policy Choices in Times of Economic Change.* Master's thesis, University of Georgia, 1993.

Fehrm, Martin. "Sweden." In *Nuclear Non-proliferation: The Why and the Wherefore,* edited by Jozef Goldblat. London: Taylor & Francis, 1985.

Field, Robert Michael. "The Growth of China's Economy, 1949–1985." In *U.S.-China Trade: Problems and Prospects,* edited by Eugene K. Lawson. New York: Praeger, 1988.

Finney, Lynne Dratler. "Development Assistance—A Tool of Foreign Policy." *Case Western Reserve Journal of International Law* 15 (spring 1983): 213–52.

Foreign Broadcast Information Service Daily Report, September 8, 1982.

Friedman, Thomas. "A Diplomatic Question: Embargo or Embrace." *New York Times,* September 4, 1994, Section E, p. 4.

Garrett, Banning, and Bonnie Glaser. "From Nixon to Reagan: China's Changing Role in American Strategy." In *Eagle Resurgent?* edited by Kenneth A. Oye, Robert J. Licher, and Donald Rothchild. Boston, MA: Little, Brown, 1987.

Garrett, Banning, and Bonnie Glaser. *War and Peace: The Views From Moscow and Beijing.* Berkeley, CA: Institute of International Studies, 1984.

Garris, Jerome H. *Sweden and the Spread of Nuclear Weapons: A Study in Restraint.* Ph.D. diss., University of California at Los Angeles, 1972.

Garver, John. "Peking's Soviet and American Policies: Toward Equidistance." *Issues and Studies* 24, no. 10 (October 1988): 55–77.

Gaventa, John. *Power and Powerlessness.* Urbana: University of Illinois Press, 1980.

"General Details Arms Production Phase-out," *Mlada Fronta.* In *East Europe,* FBIS-EEU-90–056, March 22, 1990, p. 22.

George, Alexander L. *Bridging the Gap: Theory and Practice in Foreign Policy.* Washington, DC: U.S. Institute of Peace, 1993.

George, Alexander L. "Case Studies and Theory Development." Paper presented to the second annual Symposium on Information Processing in Organizations, Carnegie Mellon University, October 15–16, 1982.

George, Alexander L., and Timothy J. McKeown. "Case Studies and Theories in

Organizational Decision-making." In *Advances in Information Processing in Organizations,* edited by B. Coulum and R. Smith. Greenwich, CT: JAI Press, 1985.

George, Alexander L., David K. Hall, and William E. Simons. *The Limits of Coercive Diplomacy.* Boston, MA: Little, Brown and Co., 1971.

Gilpin, Robert. *U.S. Power and the Multinational Corporation.* New York: Basic Books, 1975.

Gimstedt, O. "Three Decades of Nuclear Power Development in Sweden." *International Conference on Nuclear Power Experience.* Vienna: IAEA, 1983.

Goldstein, Joshua S., and John R. Freeman. *Three-Way Street: Strategic Reciprocity in World Politics.* Chicago: University of Chicago Press, 1991.

Gourevitch, Peter. "The Second Image Reversed: The International Sources of Domestic Policies." *International Organization* 32, no. 4 (autumn 1978): 881–912.

Graff, James L. "Confronting a Tankless Task." *Time,* June 17, 1991, 42.

Green, Jerrold. "Strategies for Evading Economic Sanctions." In *Dilemmas of Economic Coercion: Sanctions in World Politics,* edited by M. Nincic and P. Wallensteen. New York: Praeger, 1983.

Grieco, Joseph. *Cooperation Among Nations.* Ithaca, NY: Cornell University Press, 1990.

Grieco, Joseph. "Anarchy and the Limits of Cooperation: A Realist Critique of the Newest Liberal Institutionalism." *International Organization* 42, no. 3 (summer 1988): 485–507.

Grieco, Joseph, Robert Powell, and Duncan Snidal. "The Relative Gains Problem for International Cooperation." *American Political Science Review* 87, no. 3 (September 1993): 729–43.

Gudehus, Brigitte Schroeder. "Science, Technology Policy and Foreign Policy." In *Science, Technology and Society,* edited by Ina Spiegal-Rosing and Derek de Solla Price. Beverly Hills, CA: Sage Publications, 1977.

Halperin, Morton H. *Bureaucratic Politics and Foreign Policy.* Washington, DC: Brookings Institution, 1974.

Hamrin, Carol Lee. *China and the Challenge of the Future.* Boulder, CO: Westview Press, 1990.

Hamrin, Carol Lee. "The Impact of Politics on China's Modernization." In *U.S.-China Trade: Problems and Prospects,* edited by Eugene Lawson. New York: Praeger, 1988.

Hamrin, Carol Lee. "China Reassesses the Superpowers." *Pacific Affairs* 56, no.2 (summer 1983): 209–25.

Harding, Harry. *China's Second Revolution.* Washington, DC: Brookings Institution, 1987.

Harding, Harry, ed. *China's Foreign Relations in the 1980s.* New Haven, CT: Yale University Press, 1984.

Harsanyi, J. C. "Measurement of Social Power, Opportunity Costs, and the Theory of Two-person Bargaining Games." *Behavioral Science* (January 1962): 67–80.

Hirschman, Albert O. *National Power and the Structure of Foreign Trade.* Berkeley: University of California Press, 1980.

Ho, Samuel, and Ralph Huenemann. *China's Open Door Policy: The Quest for Foreign Technology and Capital.* Vancouver: University of British Columbia Press, 1984.

Hoffman, Fredrik. "The Functions of Economic Sanctions: A Comparative Analysis." *Journal of Peace Research* 4, no. 2 (spring 1967): 140–59.

Holst, Johan Jorgen. "Confidence-building: A Conceptual Framework." *Survival* 25, no. 1 (January/February 1983): 2–15.

Hufbauer, Gary, Jeffrey Schott, and Kimberly Ann Elliott. *Economic Sanctions Reconsidered.* Washington, DC: Institute for International Economics, 1985.

Hyland, William B. "The Sino-Soviet Conflict." In *The China Factor: Sino-American Relations and the Global Scene,* edited by Richard Solomon. Englewood Cliffs, NJ: Prentice-Hall, 1981.

Ikenberry, John. "Conclusion: An Institutional Approach to American Foreign Policy." *International Organization* 42, no. 1 (winter 1988): 219–43.

Jacobs, Stanford L. "Small Firms Upset by Effort to Limit High-Tech Exports." *Wall Street Journal,* April 4, 1983, p. 19.

Janis, Irving L., and Leon Mann. *Decision-making: A Psychological Analysis of Conflict, Choice, and Commitment.* New York: Free Press, 1977.

Jasper, James. *Nuclear Politics: Energy and the State in the United States, Sweden, and France.* Princeton, NJ: Princeton University Press, 1990.

Jervis, Robert. "Realism, Game Theory, and Cooperation." *World Politics* 40, no. 3 (April 1988): 317–49.

Jervis, Robert. "Cooperation Under the Security Dilemma." *World Politics* 30, no. 2 (January 1978): 167–214.

Jervis, Robert. *Perception and Misperception in International Politics.* Princeton, NJ: Princeton University Press, 1976.

Jervis, Robert. *The Logic of Images in International Relations.* Princeton, NJ: Princeton University Press, 1970.

Jervis, Robert. "Hypotheses on Misperception." *World Politics* 20, no. 3 (April 1968): 454–79.

Johansson, Thomas B. "Sweden's Abortive Nuclear Weapons Project." *Bulletin of the Atomic Scientists* 42, no. 3 (March 1986): 33.

Kalish, Harry I. *From Behavioral Science to Behavior Modification.* New York: McGraw-Hill Book Company, 1981.

Katzenstein, Peter. Introduction and Conclusion to "Between Power and Plenty: Foreign Economic Policies of Advanced Industrial States." *International Organization* 31, no. 4 (autumn 1977): 587–606, 879–920.

Keidel, Albert. "China's Economy in the Year 2000." In *China's Global Presence.* Washington, DC: American Enterprise Institute for Public Policy Research, 1988.

Keohane, Robert. "International Institutions: Two Approaches." *International Studies Quarterly* 32, no. 4 (December 1988): 379–96.

Keohane, Robert. *After Hegemony.* Princeton, NJ: Princeton University Press, 1984.

Kinder, Donald R., and Janet A. Weiss. "In Lieu of Rationality: Psychological

Perspectives on Foreign Policy Decision Making." *Journal of Conflict Resolution* 22, no. 4 (December 1978): 707–35.

Knopf, Jeffrey W. "Beyond Two-Level Games: Domestic-International Interaction in the INF Episode." Paper presented at the annual meeting of the American Political Science Association, Washington, DC, September 2–5, 1993.

Knorr, Klaus. *The Power of Nations.* New York: Basic Books, 1975.

Krasner, Stephen D. "Sovereignty: An Institutional Perspective." *Comparative Political Studies* 21, no. 1 (April 1988): 66–94.

Krasner, Stephen D. "Approaches to the State: Alternative Conceptualizations and Historical Dynamics." *Comparative Politics* 16, no. 2 (January 1984): 223–46.

Krasner, Stephen D. *Defending the National Interest.* Princeton, NJ: Princeton University Press, 1978.

Krasner, Stephen D. "State Power and the Structure of International Trade." *World Politics* 28, no. 3 (April 1976): 317–47.

Kriesberg, Louis. "Carrots, Sticks, De-escalation: U.S.-Soviet and Arab-Israeli Relations." *Armed Forces and Society* 13, no. 3 (spring 1987): 403–23.

Kuo, Cheng-Tian. "Formal Models of Economic Statecraft." Paper presented at the annual meeting of the International Studies Association, Acapulco, Mexico, March 24, 1993.

Lake, David A. "The State in American Trade Strategy in the Pre-Hegemonic Era." *International Organization* 42, no. 1 (winter 1988): 33–58.

Lampton, David M. "America's China Policy: Developing a Fifth Strategy." In *The China Challenge: American Politics in East Asia,* edited by Frank J. Macchiarola and Robert B. Oxnom. *Proceedings of the Academy of Political Science.* New York: (October 1991).

Larabee, Stephen, and Dietrich Stobbes, eds. *Confidence-building Measures in Europe.* New York: Institute for East-West Security Studies, 1983.

Larson, Deborah Welch. "The Psychology of Reciprocity in International Relations." *Negotiation Journal* 4, no. 3 (July 1988): 281–301.

Larsson, Christer. "History of the Swedish Atomic Bomb, 1945–1972." *Ny Teknik* (April 1985).

Lave, Charles A., and James G. March. *An Introduction to Models in the Social Sciences.* New York: Harper & Row, 1975.

Lawson, Fred. "Using Positive Sanctions to End International Conflicts: Iran and Arab Gulf Countries." *Journal of Peace Research* 20, no. 4 (1983): 311–28.

Lebow, Richard Ned. *Between Peace and War.* Baltimore, MD: Johns Hopkins University Press, 1981.

Legro, Jeffrey W. "Preferences and International Cooperation." Paper presented at the 1993 annual meeting of the American Political Science Association, Washington, DC, September 2–5, 1993.

Leng, Russell J., and Hugh G. Wheeler. "Influence Strategies, Success, and War." *Journal of Conflict Resolution* 23, no. 4 (December 1979): 655–84.

Lenway, Stephanie Ann. "Economic Sanctions and Statecraft." *International Organization* 42, no. 2 (spring 1988): 397–426.

Levy, Jack S. "Prospect Theory and International Relations: Theoretical Applications and Analytical Problems." *Political Psychology* 13, no. 2 (June 1992): 283–310.

Leyton-Brown, David, ed., *The Utility of International Economic Sanctions.* London: Croom & Helm, 1987.

Lieberthal, Kenneth. "Domestic Politics and Foreign Policy." In *China's Foreign Relations in the 1980s,* edited by Harry Harding. New Haven, CT: Yale University Press, 1984.

Lijphart, Arend. "Comparative Politics and the Comparative Method." *American Political Science Review* 65, no. 3 (September 1971): 682–93.

Lipson, Charles. "International Cooperation in Economic and Security Affairs." *World Politics* 37, no. 1 (1984): 1–23.

Liska, George. *The New Statecraft: Foreign Aid in American Foreign Policy.* Chicago: University of Chicago Press, 1960.

"List of Chemical Warfare Agents Producers Reported," *Mlada Fronta Dnes,* February 21, 1991, p. 2. In *East Europe,* FBIS-EEU-91–039, February 27, 1991, p. 22.

Long, William. *U.S. Export Control Policy: Executive Autonomy Versus Congressional Reform.* New York: Columbia University Press, 1989.

Lord, Winston. "China and America: Beyond the Big Chill." *Foreign Affairs* 68, no. 4 (fall 1989): 1–26.

Lukes, Steven. *Power: A Radical View.* London: MacMillan, 1974.

Martin, Lisa L. *Coercive Cooperation: Explaining Multilateral Economic Sanctions.* Princeton, NJ: Princeton University Press, 1992.

Mayall, James. "The Sanctions Problem in International Economic Relations." *International Affairs* 60, no. 4. (October 1984): 631–42.

McDonald, T. David. *The Technological Transformation of China.* Washington, DC: National Defense University Press, 1990.

Miko, Francis T. "Parliamentary Development in the Czech and Slovak Federal Republic." *CRS Review* (July 1991): 35–37.

"Military Cooperation Accord Signed with France," CSTK, April 13, 1992. In *East Europe,* FBIS-EEU-92–068, April 8, 1992, p. 3.

Miller, Benjamin. "Explaining Great Power Cooperation in Conflict Management." *World Politics* 45, no. 1 (October 1992): 1–46.

Milner, Helen. "International Theories of Cooperation Among Nations: Strengths and Weaknesses." *World Politics* 44, no. 3 (April 1992): 317–47.

Moe, Terry. "Interests, Institutions, and Positive Theory: The Politics of the NLRB." In *Studies in American Political Development,* vol. 2. Edited by Karen Orren and Stephen Skowronek. New Haven, CT: Yale University Press, 1987.

Monen, Paul. "China, U.S. Set Further Arms Buy Talks." *Aviation Week and Space Technology* (June 11, 1984): 22–23.

Moravcsik, Andrew. "Preferences and Power in the European Community: A Liberal Intergovernmentalist Approach." *Journal of Common Market Studies* 31 (October 1993): 29–80.

Morganthau, Hans J. *Politics Among Nations, 5th ed.* New York: Alfred A. Knopf, 1978.

Mortellaro, Joseph. "Normalization and Subsequent Sino-American Economic Relations." *Asian Profile* 13 (1985): 299–306.

Mullenbach, Philip. *Civilian Nuclear Power: Economic Issues and Policy Formulation.* New York: Twentieth Century Fund, 1963.

"National Assembly Approves Arms Agreements," CTK, March 19, 1991. In *East Europe,* FBIS-EEU-91–054, March 20, 1993, p. 25.

Nations, Richard. "Who's in Charge Here?" *Far Eastern Economic Review* 120, no. 14 (April 7, 1983): 28–29.

Nelson, Joan M. *Aid, Influence and Foreign Policy.* New York: Macmillan, 1968.

"New Guidelines Set For Exports to China." *Business America* (October 6, 1980), p. 20.

Nieburg, H. L. *Nuclear Secrecy and Foreign Policy.* Washington, DC: Public Affairs Press, 1964.

"No Objections to Total Ban on Chemical Weapons," *Svbodne Slovo,* October 25, 1990, p. 2. In *East Europe,* FBIS-EEU-90–212, November 1, 1990, p. 18.

"Note by the Executive Secretary of the National Security Council (Souers), on the United States Policy Regarding Trade with China." *FRUS 1949* 9 (February 28, 1949): 826–34.

Nye, Joseph, Jr. "Neo-realism and Neo-liberalism." *World Politics* 40, no. 2 (January 1988): 235–51.

Nye, Joseph, Jr. "Nuclear Learning and U.S.-Soviet Security Regimes." *International Organization* 41, no. 3 (summer 1987): 371–402.

Obey, David, and Carol Lancaster. "Funding Foreign Aid." *Foreign Policy,* no. 71 (summer 1988): 141–55.

"OECD Report Praises CSFR for Rapid Economic Progress." *International Trade Reporter* (January 8, 1992): 69.

"Official on Production of Armaments," CTK, June 20, 1990. In *East Europe,* FBIS-EEU-90–121, June 22, 1990, p. 20.

Oksenberg, Michael. "A Decade of Sino-American Relations." *Foreign Affairs* 61, no. 1 (1982): 175–95.

Olmer, Lionel H., and William J. Long. "Setting Technology Export Thresholds." In *Law and Policy of Export Controls,* edited by Homer Moyer et al. Washington, DC: American Bar Association Press, 1993.

Pehe, Jiri, ed. "Czechoslovakia in a New International Context." *Radio Free Europe/Radio Liberty Research Report* 1, no. 16 (April 1992): 30.

"People's Republic of China; Export Control Policy; Placement in Country Group V," *Federal Register* 48 (1983): 53,064–71.

Pilat, Joseph F., Robert E. Pendley, and Charles K. Ebinger, eds. *Atoms for Peace: An Analysis After Thirty Years.* Boulder, CO: Westview Press, 1983.

Pillsbury, Michael. "U.S.-Chinese Military Ties?" *Foreign Policy* 20 (fall 1975): 50–64.

Pollack, Jonathan. "China and the Global Strategic Balance." In *China's Foreign Relations in the 1980s,* edited by Harry Harding. New Haven, CT: Yale University Press, 1984.

Polsby, Nelson W. *Congress and the Presidency.* Englewood Cliffs, NJ: Prentice Hall, 1973.

Potter, William C. *Nuclear Power and Nonproliferation.* Cambridge, MA: Oelgeschlager, Gunn, and Hain, 1982.

Pravda, March 9, 1980, reprinted in part, *Washington Post,* March 10, 1980, Section A, p. 16.

Prawitz, Jan. "Sweden—A Non-Nuclear Weapon State." In *Security, Order, and the Bomb,* edited by Johan Jorgan Holst. Oslo: Universitetsforlaget, 1972.

"President Bush December 6 Lifted U.S. Arms Embargoes." *International Trade Reporter* (December 11, 1991): 1827.

President Bush, U.S. Department of State. Dispatch. 1991. "Czechoslovakia: From Revolution to Renaissance." Washington, DC.

"President Signs Measure Extending Permanent MFN to Hungary, CSFR." *International Trade Reporter* (April 15, 1992): 700.

Press Briefing by Secretary of State Warren Christopher and Secretary of Treasury Lloyd Benson, Okura Hotel, Tokyo, Japan, July 7, 1993.

Putnam, Robert. "Diplomacy and Domestic Politics: The Logic of Two-Level Games." *International Organization* 42, no. 3 (summer 1988): 427–60.

Quester, George. *The Politics of Nuclear Proliferation.* Baltimore: Johns Hopkins University Press, 1973.

Qingshan, Tan. *The Making of U.S. China Policy.* Boulder, CO: Lynn Rienner Publishers, 1992.

Qiwei, Chen. "Why is China Opening to the Outside?" *Beijing Review* (April 1, 1985): 18–22.

Raser, John R. "Learning and Affect in International Politics." *Journal of Peace Research* 2, no. 3 (summer 1965): 216–27.

Ray, Edward John. "Changing Patterns of Protection: The Fall in Tariffs and the Rise in Non-Tariff Barriers." *Northwestern Journal of International Law and Business* 8 (1987): 286–326.

Reiss, Mitchell. *Without the Bomb: The Politics of Nuclear Nonproliferation.* New York: Columbia University Press, 1988.

"Report Prepared by the Economic Cooperation Administration." *FRUS 1951* 7 (February 1951): 1907–1910.

Ross, Madelyn C. "Export Controls: Where China Fits In." *China Business Review* 11, no. 3 (May–June 1984): 58.

Rowe, David M. "The Domestic Political Economy of International Economic Sanctions." Paper presented at the annual meeting of the American Political Science Association, Washington, DC, September 2–5, 1993, pp. 8–11.

Scheinman, Lawrence. "The Pendulum Swings While the Clock Ticks." In *The Nonproliferation Predicament,* edited by Joseph F. Pilat. New Brunswick: Transaction Books, 1985.

Schelling, Thomas C. *Arms and Influence.* New Haven, CT: Yale University Press, 1966.

Schlesinger, James R. "Atoms for Peace Revisited." In *Atoms for Peace: An Analysis After Thirty Years,* edited by Joseph F. Pilat, Robert E. Pendley, and Charles K. Ebinger. Boulder, CO: Westview Press, 1983.

Schreiber, Anna P. "Economic Coercion as an Instrument of Policy: U.S. Measures Against Cuba and the Dominican Republic." *World Politics* 25, no. 3 (April 1973): 387–413.

Seabolt, D. Grant. "United States Technology Exports to the People's Republic of China: Current Developments in Law and Policy." *Texas International Law Journal* 19, no. 3 (summer 1984): 599–600.

Seaborg, Glenn. "Travels in the New World." Washington, DC, 1972.

Selected Works of Mao Zedong, vol. 4. Beijing: People's Publishing House, 1968.

Shanghai Joint Communiqué. *Weekly Compiled Presidential Documents* 8 (February 28, 1972): 473.

Simon, Herbert A. *Administrative Behavior.* New York: Free Press, 1946.

"Small Arms Exports to Proposed," CTK, April 15, 1991. In *East Europe,* FBIS-EEU-91–074, April 17, 1991, p. 10.

Snidal, Duncan. "International Cooperation Among Relative Gain Maximizers." *International Studies Quarterly* 35, no. 4 (December 1991): 387–402.

Solow, Robert M. "Technological Change and the Aggregate Production Function." *Review of Economics and Statistics* 39 (1957): 312–20.

Stein, Arthur. *Why Nations Cooperate.* Ithaca, NY: Cornell University Press, 1990.

Stein, Arthur. "When Misperception Matters." *World Politics* 34, no. 4 (July 1982): 505–26.

Steinbrunner, John. *The Cybernetic Theory of Decision: New Dimensions of Political Analysis.* Princeton, NJ: Princeton University Press, 1974.

Suchanek, Milan. "Nations Urged to Heed Example, End Arms Export," Radio Prague, January 16. In *East Europe,* FBIS-EEU-90–025. February 6, 1990, pp. 12–13.

Sullivan, Roger. "The Nature and Implications of United States–China Trade Toward the Year 2000." In *China's Global Presence,* edited by David Lampton and Katherine Keyser. Washington, DC: American Enterprise Institute, 1988.

Sutter, Robert G. *Sino-Soviet Relations: Recent Improvements and Implications for the United States.* Library of Congress, Issue Brief, 86138, 1986.

Sutter, Robert G. "Realities of International Power and China's 'Interdependence' in Foreign Affairs." *Journal of Northeast Asian Studies* 3, no. 4 (winter 1984): 3–28.

Sutter, Robert G. *The China Quandary: Domestic Determinants of U.S. China Policy, 1972–1982.* Boulder, CO: Westview Press, 1983.

Svek, Milan. "Czechoslovakia's Velvet Divorce." *Current History* 91 (November 1992): 376–80.

Synder, Glenn H., and Paul Diesing. *Conflict Among Nations: Bargaining, Decision Making, and System Structure in International Crises.* Princeton, NJ: Princeton University Press, 1977.

Szitek, Ivan. "An Assessment: Czechoslovak Economic Reform in 1991." *Radio Free Europe/Radio Liberty Research Report* 1, no. 21 (May 1992): 46.

Tape, Gerald F. "Historical and Political Framework of Safeguards," reprinted in U.S. House. Subcommittee on Energy Research and Production of the Committee on Science and Technology. *Nuclear Safeguards: A Reader.* 98th Cong., 1st sess., December 1983.

Tape, Gerald F. "The Fabric of Cooperation." In *Atoms for Peace: An Analysis After Thirty Years,* edited by Joseph F. Pilat, Robert E. Pendley, and Charles K. Ebinger. Boulder, CO: Westview Press, 1983.

"Telegram from the Department of State to the Permanent Representative at the North Atlantic Council." *FRUS 1955–57* 10 (October 1, 1955): 255–56.

"Telegram from the Office of the Permanent Representative at the North Atlantic Council to the Department of State." *FRUS 1955–57* 10 (October 6, 1955): 259–62.

Truman, David. *The Governmental Process: Political Interests and Public Opinion.* New York: Knopf, 1971.

Tsao, James. *China's Development Strategies and Foreign Trade.* Lexington, MA: Lexington Books, 1987.

"Turning to Tanks to Fill the Till." *Business Week* (July 12, 1993): 20.

U.S. Atomic Energy Commission 1954, *International Cooperation in the Peaceful Uses of Atomic Energy Through the Instrument of the Bilateral Agreement for Cooperation,* republished in U.S. Congress, Joint Committee on Atomic Energy. *Background Information for the Review of the International Atomic Policies and Programs of the United States,* vol. 2, 80th Cong., 2d sess., October 1960.

U.S. Central Intelligence Agency, Technology Transfer Assessment Center, "Soviet Requirements for Western Technology," Washington, DC, 1987. unpublished.

U.S. Congress. House. Committee on Foreign Relations. *Approval of Extension of Most-Favored-Nation Treatment to Czechoslovakia.* 101st Cong., 2d sess., November 15, 1990.

U.S. Congress. House. Committee on Foreign Relations. *United States and the People's Republic of China: Issues for the 1980s. Hearings before the Subcommittee on Asian and Pacific Affairs.* 96th Cong., 2d sess., 1980.

U.S. Congress. House. Committee on Foreign Relations. *United States-China Relations: A Strategy for the Future; Hearings before the Committee on Foreign Relations, Subcommittee on Asian and Pacific Affairs.* 91st Cong., 2d sess., 1970.

U.S. Congress. House. Committee on Foreign Relations. *Mutual Defense Assistance Control Act of 1951 (Battle Act): Hearings before the Committee on Foreign Relations.* 82nd Cong., 1st sess., 1951.

U.S. Congress. Joint Economic Committee. *China Under the Four Modernizations,* Part 1, 97th Cong., 2d sess., August 13, 1982.

U.S. Congress. Senate. Committee on Foreign Relations. *U.S. Policy with Respect to Mainland China: Hearings before the Committee on Foreign Relations.* 89th Cong., 2d sess., 1966.

U.S. Congress. Senate. Committee on Governmental Affairs, Subcommittee on Investigations. *Conversion of Arms Industry in Central Europe.* 102 Cong., 2d sess., 1991.

U.S. Congress. Senate. *Extension of Non-Discriminatory Treatment to Products of the Czech and Slovak Federal Republic,* 101st Cong., 2d sess., January 14, 1991.

"U.S.-C.S.F.R. Bilateral Agreement on Investments to Take Force December 19." *International Trade Reporter* (December 9, 1993): 2105.

U.S. Department of Commerce. *Export Administration Report.* Washington, DC: Government Printing Office, 1991.

U.S. Department of Defense. Secretary of Defense Memorandum from Robert McNamara to President John Kennedy, "The Diffusion of Nuclear Weapons With and Without a Test Ban Treaty," February 12, 1963.

U.S. Department of Labor. "Productivity and the Economy." *Bulletin of the Bureau of Labor Statistics,* no. 1926. Washington, DC: Government Printing Office, 1977.

U.S. Department of State. Bureau of Intelligence and Research. "Swedish Government Initiates Nuclear Weapons Research," *Intelligence Report,* no. 8223, February 12, 1960.

U.S. Department of State. Memorandum of Howard A. Robinson for Gerald C. Smith, "European Perspectives on Recent American Moves in the Field of Atomic Energy." October 21, 1954.

U.S. International Trade Commission, *29th Quarterly Report to Congress and the Trade Policy Committee on Trade Between the U.S. and the Non-Market Countries During 1981.* Washington, DC: International Trade Commission, 1982.

U.S. National Security Council. Document 5507/2, "Statement of Policy on Peaceful Uses of Atomic Energy, General Considerations," March 12, 1955.

U.S. Office of Technology Assessment, *Technology Transfer to China.* Washington, DC: Government Printing Office, July 1987.

"U.S., Other Nations Reach Agreement on Restricting Nuclear Weapons Exports." *International Trade Reporter* (March 11, 1992): 435.

"USTR Adds 83 Eastern European Products to GSP List Resulting From Special Review." *International Trade Reporter* (June 17, 1992): 1053.

"U.S. Welcomes COCOM Decision to Relax Controls on High-Tech Exports to Hungary." *International Trade Reporter* (May 6, 1992): 791.

"U.S. Will Continue Providing Aid to Dividend CSFR, Official Says." *International Trade Reporter* (August 5, 1992): 1352.

Vance, Cyrus. *Hard Choices: Critical Years in American Foreign Policy.* New York: Simon and Schuster, 1983.

von Amerongen, Otto Wolff. "Economic Sanctions as a Foreign Policy Tool?" *International Security* 5 (fall 1980): 159–67.

Wagner, R. Harrison. "Economic Interdependence, Bargaining Power, and Political Influence." *International Organization* 42, no. 3 (summer 1988): 461–83.

Wagner, R. Harrison. "The Theory of Games and the Problem of International Cooperation." *American Political Science Review* 77 (June 1983): 330–46.

Walker, William, and Måns Lonnroth. *Nuclear Power Struggles.* London: Allen and Unwin, 1983.

Wallenstein, Peter. "Characteristics of Economic Sanctions." *Journal of Peace Research* 5, no. 3 (summer 1968): 248–67.

Wallerstein, Mitchel B., ed. *Scientific and Technological Cooperation among Advanced Industrialized Countries: The Role of the United States.* Washington, DC: National Academy Press, 1984.

Wallin, Lars. "Sweden." In *Security with Nuclear Weapons: Different Perspectives on National Security,* edited by Regina Cowen Karp. Stockholm: Stockholm International Peace Research Institute and Oxford University Press, 1991.

Waltz, Kenneth. *The Spread of Nuclear Weapons: More May be Better.* Adelphi Paper no. 171. London: International Institute for Strategic Studies, 1981.

Waltz, Kenneth. *Theory of International Politics.* Reading, MA: Addison-Wesley, 1979.

Weisskopf, Michael. "Chinese Trade Issues Seen Snagging Schultz." *Washington Post,* January 31, 1983, Section A, p.12.

Wendt, Alexander. "The Agent-Structure Problem in International Relations Theory." *International Organization* 41, no. 3 (summer 1987): 335–70.

Wendt, Allen. "U.S. Export Controls in a Changing Global Environment." *U.S. Department of State Dispatch* (July 1, 1991): 480–82.

Willrich, Mason. *Non-Proliferation Treaty: Framework for Nuclear Arms Control.* Charlottesville, VA: Michie Company, 1969.

Wolchik, Sharon L. "The Politics of Eastern Europe's Move to the Market." *Current History* 91 (November 1992): 390–94.

World Military Expenditures and Arms Transfers. Washington, DC: Government Printing Office, 1989–90.

Woodward, Kim. *The International Energy Relations of China.* Stanford, CA: Stanford University Press, 1980.

Yuan, Jing-dong. "Between Economic Warfare and Strategic Embargo: U.S.-U.K. Conflicts over Export Controls on the PRC, 1949–1957." *Issues and Studies* 30, no. 3 (March 1994): 80–86.

Zagoria, Donald. "The Moscow-Beijing Détente." *Foreign Affairs* 61, no. 4 (spring 1983): 853–73.

Zimmerman, Robert F. *Dollars, Diplomacy, and Dependency: Dilemmas of U.S. Economic Aid.* Boulder, CO: Lynne Rienner, 1993.

Index